From CHARM to HARM:

The Guide to Spotting, Naming, and Stopping Emotional Abuse in Intimate Relationships

AMY LEWIS BEAR

BALBOA.PRESS
A DIVISION OF HAY HOUSE

Balboa Press books may be ordered through booksellers or by contacting:

Balboa Press
A Division of Hay House
1663 Liberty Drive
Bloomington, IN 47403
www.balboapress.com
844-682-1282

Because of the dynamic nature of the Internet, any web addresses or
links contained in this book may have changed since publication and
may no longer be valid. The views expressed in this work are solely those
of the author and do not necessarily reflect the views of the publisher,
and the publisher hereby disclaims any responsibility for them.

The author of this book does not dispense medical advice or prescribe the use
of any technique as a form of treatment for physical, emotional, or medical
problems without the advice of a physician, either directly or indirectly. The
intent of the author is only to offer information of a general nature to help
you in your quest for emotional and spiritual well-being. In the event you use
any of the information in this book for yourself, which is your constitutional
right, the author and the publisher assume no responsibility for your actions.

Any people depicted in stock imagery provided by Getty Images are
models, and such images are being used for illustrative purposes only.
Certain stock imagery © Getty Images.

Print information available on the last page.

ISBN: 978-1-4525-9159-9 (sc)
ISBN: 978-1-4525-9161-2 (hc)
ISBN: 978-1-4525-9160-5 (e)

Library of Congress Control Number: 2014901985

Balboa Press rev. date: 01/05/2024

Illustrations by Joseph Benjamin Brown

To all the courageous women and men I've known who stood up to abusive partners and claimed their right to be in respectful, loving relationships. They helped themselves and others by speaking out about their experiences and inspired me to write this book.

Contents

Part II – Emotional Abuse Tactics, Effects, and Contributors

Part III – Assessment, Protection, and Treatment

PREFACE

GENDER AND EMOTIONAL ABUSE IN INTIMATE RELATIONSHIPS

From Charm to Harm focuses on emotional abuse in intimate relationships. Research shows that when abuse occurs in heterosexual relationships, it is most often men who abuse their female partners. For that reason, most of the anecdotes and illustrations in this book depict heterosexual relationships with the male as the abuser. But women can abuse men. Likewise, a partner in a same-sex relationship can be an abuser. Many of the terms I have used can be applied to emotional abuse between any two people.

INCIDENCE OF EMOTIONAL ABUSE IN AMERICA

The National Coalition Against Domestic Violence uncovered an epidemic of domestic violence in the United States. Its research shows that one in every four women will experience physical violence in her lifetime. Emotional abuse is the greatest predictor of physical abuse. Where there is physical abuse, there is always emotional abuse, but the opposite is not necessarily true. Emotional abuse is difficult to define or prove, but it's reasonable to assume that emotional abuse has also reached epidemic proportions.

How to Use This Book

From Charm to Harm is divided into three parts. The first part provides a bird's-eye view of what it's like to live in an emotionally abusive relationship from the abused person's perspective. The emotional abuse tactics, effects, and contributors in the story of Susan and Jack are listed after the epilogue with page numbers for reference. Part one also includes an overview of emotional abuse that helps explain how and why it happens.

The second part and main portion of the book provides a language to describe specific emotional abuse tactics, effects, and contributors. The tactics are in one section, and the effects and contributors are in another because they are interchangeable. Both sections are categorized into subheadings for easier location.

Each tactic, effect, and contributor is described with a word or phrase, definition, word variation, and brief scene. The word variations of nouns, verbs, and adjectives make the tactics, effects, and contributors easier to describe in conversation. Many of the terms are illustrated to help readers visualize the descriptions.

Flip through the book and find the right word, definition, and scene to identify and explain emotional abuse and its effects and contributors in relationships.

The third and final part of *From Charm to Harm* will help you to determine if your partner is emotionally abusive to you, how the abuse effects you, and how you may be contributing to your partner's maltreatment. The three quizzes will increase your awareness about the dynamics and power balance in your relationship. The section also contains ways to protect yourself from an abusive mate and what to do if you decide to leave the relationship,

If you are seeking treatment for you or your mate, you will find useful information on how to find the right psychotherapist and what to expect from individual and group psychotherapy. Complete the book's quizzes and take them to your psychotherapist to get a jump start on treatment.

Use the book to get support from family and friends by helping them comprehend the hidden nature of emotional abuse. Share the book with loved ones who are emotionally battered. Help teenagers and young adults be alert to the hazards of involvement with an abusive person.

If you are in the process of divorce, take the book to your legal representatives to educate them about your abusive mate, so they can better represent you.

Clinicians can use the book as a therapeutic tool to help clients gain deeper insight into their experience with abuse and work toward recovery. Greater awareness of past relationships can help avoid future involvement with an abusive person.

Warning: *From Charm to Harm* may cause grief reactions in readers who have lived with emotional abuse or experienced it through a loved one. Symptoms such as deep sadness, irritability, sleep disturbance, and lack of concentration may occur. Psychosomatic reactions can include headaches, nausea, or gastric distress. Please know that help exists for you. See a counselor, use community resources, or seek support from your loved ones.

ACKNOWLEDGMENTS

During the past thirty years of learning about emotional abuse, I've had many teachers. They include hundreds of emotional abuse survivors I've treated in individual and group therapy, numerous friends and acquaintances who shared their stories, and, ironically, my own past relationships with emotionally abusive people.

There are others whose support and encouragement led me to write this book:

Psychotherapist Richard Gerson provided me with the crucial opportunity to work in a psychiatric hospital, where I learned what can happen to those who are abused by people who are supposed to love them.

Psychologist Dr. David Lane and psychiatrist Dr. Stephen Howard broadened my knowledge of psychotherapy practice with their experience, guidance, and considerable wisdom. I had the good fortune to be a member of their psychotherapy supervision groups early in my career.

Psychotherapist Cheri Augustine Flake always stepped up at the right moment to help me fulfill my dream to become a psychotherapist.

Psychotherapist Lauren Crawford Taylor generously gave me her support and advice, which enabled me to build a private practice.

Psychologist Dr. Pati Beaudoin, with the Institute for Clarity, saw the potential in my book idea and urged me to write the book.

Along the way, she graciously shared her professional expertise and made important contributions to the book.

Margot Swann and her team at Visions Anew Institute helped me cross paths with hundreds of women who deepened my expertise in treating emotional abuse survivors.

Editor Bobbie Christmas provided encouragement, useful editorial suggestions, and books she authored on writing technique.

Treasured friends cheered me on and gave me great ideas: Lee Ayers, Francine Carlin, Phyllis Carrera, Patti Cochran, JoAnne Donner, Ray Harbor, Marcia Jaffe, and Susan Reinstein Rice.

My extended family of Bears, Glassers, Levensteims, and Siegels warmly welcomed my son and me when I married their uncle. Their open arms brought us into a colorful and loving family that quickly became our own.

A special thanks to my sister, Fay Leo, and brother, Roy Lewis, and their respective partners and children for their love and loyalty.

My extraordinary parents, Roy and Gloria Lewis, did their best to send me off from the starting gate prepared and ready to take on life as an adult. They have been steadfast supporters of mine ever since.

Finally, my deepest love and gratitude to my husband, Jay, and my son, Thomas. Each in his own way has provided me daily with joyful reminders of what it's like to have loving relationships.

INTRODUCTION

Emotional abuse happens when one person uses psychological intimidation to gain control over another for personal gain. The aggressor uses both obvious and hidden tactics to manipulate the other's feelings and behaviors. Abuse occurs when one person is vulnerable to another, such as in families, between friends and work colleagues, and in every other social and cultural environment where people have relationships. Emotional abuse crosses all boundaries of age, gender, race, culture, religion, socioeconomic status, and sexual orientation.

Everyone knows that ugly, offensive words and harsh voices are verbally abusive. In intimate relationships, however, the hallmark of emotional abuse is systematic deception. Abusers deliver their punches under the cover of words and actions that disguise the abuser's true intention, which is to degrade the other's self-esteem and take control. People on the receiving end of the abuse don't easily see the abuser's campaign of degradation against them. Confused and unaware, they attribute the discord to the aggressor's personality traits or their own inadequacies. They respond with an endless quest to appease the dominant one and get back into his or her good graces, which contributes to the abuse. Victims disregard themselves and risk the loss of their emotional health and well-being.

In nourishing relationships, the partners may argue, criticize each other, and, yes, use emotionally abusive language, but wrongdoers know their behavior is hurtful and inappropriate. They feel remorse, have meaningful discourse, and make genuine efforts to improve. In emotionally abusive relationships, abusers rarely exhibit true repentance. They may issue apologies, but they don't follow through with actions that prove their sincerity. They stand firm in their justification to do whatever it takes to fulfill their own unhealthy needs and desires.

A WAY TO IDENTIFY AND DESCRIBE EMOTIONAL ABUSE

Emotional abuse stays under the radar in private lives and public perception. It builds on a tragic lack of understanding about its psychological origins and schemes. It feeds on misguided social values, popular media, and, in heterosexual couples, age-old beliefs about women's inferiority to men. It passes down through generations of dysfunctional family paradigms and leaves walking wounded in its wake. Appropriate intervention is uncommon, so it thrives.

The lack of language to identify and describe emotional abuse and its aftermath is a major barrier to recognition and treatment. *From Charm to Harm* breaks down this barrier by providing simple words and definitions that name and define harmful psychological interactions between intimate partners. Many of those interactions are difficult to distinguish from the normal experience of being in a relationship.

Readers are empowered to recognize, explain, and protect themselves from emotional destruction in their intimate partnerships, and get help for both partners. They will realize that knowledge, courage, and productive action can result in positive change.

The book's content is drawn from my personal experience and my work as a psychotherapist in treating hundreds of emotional abuse survivors in individual and group therapy. The anecdotal stories are true, although I have changed or omitted identifying information for confidentiality.

Some of the tactics, effects, and contributors seem similar or repetitive; however, a closer look will reveal nuances and differing angles.

Physical and sexual abuse is often present in emotionally abusive relationships, so a section of the book briefly covers these topics.

Although emotional abuse often includes the use of profanity and vulgar language against a partner, I leave out offensive words. My intention is to avoid retraumatizing the abused and make the book more suitable for teenagers and young adults.

Some abusers use many of the tactics in this book; others use only a few, and the levels of severity can vary.

In any case, if abusive partners repeat and deny the tactics, and make light of the effects of these tactics on their partners, the relationship is emotionally abusive.

My research and experience show that the tactics, effects, and contributors in emotionally abusive relationships are remarkably consistent among people from every walk of life. I've compiled some of the major ones here, but the list is by no means complete. Abusive men and women are creative in their methods of harm, and the fallout is immense. At the end of the book, I invite readers to contribute their own experiences for future editions.

EMOTIONAL ABUSE TACTICS, EFFECTS, AND CONTRIBUTORS

The maneuvers emotionally abusive people use on their partners can be referred to as *tactics* because they are a means to an end. The tactics are used to manipulate another's thinking, feelings, and behavior in an effort to gain control over them. Some of the tactics are subconscious and others are intentional. All of the tactics cause harm.

People don't normally choose to get involved with an abusive partner, but if they find themselves in an abusive relationship, the partnership works both ways. Those who are on the receiving end of abusive tactics get caught up in an oppressive cycle. They suffer from the effects of the abuse and unwittingly contribute to it, usually by tolerating the abuse in an effort to keep the peace or improve the relationship. They may even take the blame for the abuse. In many cases, the abused are not fully aware of their contributions to the abuse, because they are in a "love" relationship, where trust is often given freely before it is deserved. They may not realize that their abusive mates see tolerance as an invitation for more of the same mistreatment.

As you read through the emotional abuse tactics, effects, and contributors in *From Charm to Harm*, you will see how they are linked and interchangeable through a cause and effect dynamic. Some of the effects from emotional abuse tactics happen before the abused make any contributions to the abuse. Most of the effects, however, are the result of tolerating—and thus contributing—to the abuse.

Part I

THE WHATS, HOWS, AND WHYS OF EMOTIONAL ABUSE

CHAPTER ONE

How Emotional Abuse Happens and How It Feels

INTRODUCTION TO THE STORY OF SUSAN AND JACK

Emotional abuse is sneaky, cumulative, and dangerous. Its tentacles wrap around you when you get involved with someone who has a deep-seated need to control you.

Let's say you're a woman who gets involved with a man. He piques your interest with his charm, looks, and ingenuity. He pursues you with an intensity you've never experienced. He makes you feel loved and special. You are certain he has the character traits you've searched for in a life partner. You return his love and feel hopeful about your future together.

Like tiny snowballs rolling downhill that cause an avalanche, indicators appear early in the relationship, but you ignore them. If you don't, he explains them away. He may falsely accuse you of cheating. He may scold you for not spending enough time with him. He may tell you he needs a partner who "has his back," and you're not living up to the job. You are confused when he makes you feel like an idiot without actually saying the word. You doubt yourself when he discounts your feelings and says you are too sensitive. You think you need to improve yourself, because according to him, you are the problem. But the more you do to earn his love, the less secure you feel in the relationship.

What you don't realize is that your lover has zeroed in on your psychological weak spots. He is taking advantage of your vulnerability to break you down and mold you into a person who meets his unwholesome wants and wishes. An overriding need to dominate others, and possibly a sense of entitlement, drives his abusive behavior, but he's indifferent to your feelings.

Regardless of his motivation, he is like a spider that catches prey in its web and paralyzes the prey before eating it. He disarms your ability to defend yourself and consumes bits and pieces of you for his own gratification.

His arsenal consists of power plays, deception, denial, invalidation, ridicule, and contradiction. These powerful weapons distort your reality, break down your intuition and judgment, and make you even more susceptible to his tactics. They cause you to feel self-doubt, shame, and guilt, and rob you of your ability to think and act spontaneously, as you would normally. Stress and anxiety envelope you, and depression creeps in.

In an effort to restore the relationship to its former glory, you think and behave in ways that contribute to the abuse. You go against your principles and put your self-respect on the line, because your only objective is to win back his love.

When with friends and family, you enter a silent conspiracy with your abusive partner to smooth over the turbulence in your relationship. Even if you want to disclose what's happening, you can't explain it. You are left alone and vulnerable to an insidious force that ravages you from the inside out as you struggle to define, or even identify, the cause.

You either disappear into the murky undertow of your union or find the strength to pull your weakened self out of the relationship. Unless you understand the whats, hows, and whys of the experience that caused you exquisite pain, you fall back into the same quagmire with another abusive partner.

Read on to see how emotional abuse happens in the story of Susan and Jack. The story is a compilation that is drawn from the true experiences of emotional abuse survivors, but the names and circumstances have been changed to protect identities.

Jack uses at least fifty-two emotional abuse tactics on Susan. Most are hidden, but Susan is unsure of even the most obvious tactics, because she sees Jack as a man who loves her and would never intentionally harm her.

Jack's abuse is particularly damaging to Susan because she is deeply conflicted about why she feels anguish, and she struggles to understand who is at fault for the strife in their marriage. She experiences twenty-six emotional abuse effects and contributors.

After you read the story, refer to the listed page numbers to read about the abuse tactics, effects, and contributors in the story. You will see how Jack's tactics increase his control over Susan by chipping away at her self-esteem and how she unknowingly contributes to his abuse.

As you learn the language of emotional abuse, you can write your own story. When you revisit your memories, you may gain clarity about your reasons for getting involved with an emotional abuser and why you stayed in a relationship so damaging to your sense of self-worth. Many of us who have been in emotionally abusive relationships know that recognition of abuse tactics, their effects, and how we contribute to the abuse, even in hindsight, is essential to end abuse and heal from the experience. Refer to page 203 for an invitation to share your story.

THE STORY OF SUSAN AND JACK

A familiar wave of heat rose from the pit of Susan's stomach and flushed her face with humiliation. She paused to collect herself and managed to smile at friends gathered around her dining room table. "Excuse me. I ... uh ... I'll be right back," she stammered as she turned away. She hurried down the hallway, slipped into the bathroom, and locked herself in.

Susan's tears brimmed and spilled down her cheeks. She questioned herself. *Why can't I be clever enough to think of a witty retort when Jack puts me down? He said it was just a joke.*

Susan had worked for two days to delight her friends with a gourmet meal and prove her culinary skills to Jack. He waited until she began to serve dinner, the crucial moment when his remark would hurt her most. "Poor Susan," he said. "She tries her best to cook, but unfortunately, she just doesn't have it. Eat at your own risk." He sneered.

The remark played over and over in her head, punctuated by Jack's usual response when his "jokes" upset her. "You're too sensitive. Don't take things so seriously."

Susan and Jack had become inseparable three years earlier when she met him through her work. His charm, intelligence, and sense of humor wooed her on their first date. Susan's interest in Jack grew as he showered her with gifts and attention. He made her feel special.

Jack impressed her with his openness when he disclosed that his "crazy" ex-wife had cheated on him multiple times. He stood by his ex-wife until his misery forced him to divorce her, but he supported her financially because he didn't want to cause her hardship. "What a decent guy," Susan gushed to her friends.

Optimism, persistence, and enthusiasm for accommodating others were among Susan's best qualities. She made roasted chicken for picnics in the park, played Jack's favorite music, and surprised him with tickets to plays and concerts. He deserved happiness after his disastrous marriage. She couldn't believe her luck in finding a man who was so vibrant, unselfish, and kindhearted.

The careers of both Jack and Susan flourished. He owned a growing medical products company, and she won praise for her work as a physician's assistant in a nonprofit hospital. Susan sensed that they shared common interests and that Jack might be the kind of man with whom she could spend her life. When she introduced him to her family and friends, everyone raved about him. He radiated geniality and graciousness. They told Susan that she and Jack exemplified a well-matched couple, and they teased her about not letting him get away.

Susan bragged to her friends about Jack's strong character traits, saying they were typical for a successful entrepreneur. She told them he flattered her when he showed an unusual interest in the details of her daily life. He wanted to know where she went, what she did, and all about her friends and coworkers. Susan didn't mind when he analyzed her decisions and told her where she went wrong. She liked a take-charge kind of guy. A friend cautioned, "Slow down. This man could be trouble," but Susan knew that Jack meant well.

Several months after Susan met Jack, he kept pressing her to move in with him, until she relented. Her intuition told her to wait and get to know Jack better, but she predicted that living together would strengthen their relationship. Jack told her he had searched for a woman like her for a long time. He loved her so much that he wanted to be with her every day.

After they moved in together, Jack and Susan went on a vacation to a beach resort near Jack's hometown. At the end of a serene day, they dined on the hotel veranda in the midst of pink and yellow hibiscus and a beautiful ocean panorama. Susan bathed in excitement for the promising life ahead of her.

Toward the end of dinner, Jack left the table twice. Susan spotted him in the bar area. He returned to pay the bill, escorted Susan back to their hotel room, and left for a long walk on the beach to "burn off all the calories." In one hour, Susan called Jack's cell phone, but he didn't answer. Two hours later, he returned and went straight into the bathroom to shower.

Susan rubbed her forehead, got out of bed, and knocked on the bathroom door. "Where have you been? I've been worried about you," she called through the door.

Jack opened the door and grimaced at her. "How can you question me after we've been together for three days straight? I needed some time alone," he protested. Jack shut the door and turned on the shower, which indicated the end of their dialogue.

Susan twisted her mouth and slumped into a chair. She grabbed her book, but thoughts nagged at her. *Is Jack unreasonable? Maybe I should forget about what happened and give him space. Was he with someone else? He may have run into an old girlfriend. No; he wouldn't do that. If he'd only answered my call, I wouldn't have worried about him.*

Jack finished his shower and went to bed. Susan hid in her book. When she heard him snoring lightly, she raised her head from the lamplight and peered into the darkened room at his muscular, tanned body. As the minutes wore on, her anger thawed. She conceded that Jack deserved time alone and put aside her grievances. How could she be irked at him for turning his phone off while he enjoyed a moonlit walk on the beach?

In the weeks after they returned home, Jack brought her flowers and called her from work to see if she needed groceries. On Saturday, he asked her for a list of things she wanted done around the house, and he completed them by the end of the weekend. Jack's thoughtfulness reinforced Susan's confidence that they were meant to be together.

As her emotional commitment to him deepened, another distressful incident occurred. Late one day, Jack told her to cancel her plans to go out with her girlfriends that evening and accompany him to a business-related event at a local nightclub. He explained that her presence would be important to his work. When she hesitated, he said, "Now that we're together, things aren't just about you anymore." Susan agreed to go with him.

At the reception, Jack left Susan with people she didn't know. She found him later in a dark corner of the bar with his arm around the young daughter of a business colleague. They were engrossed in flirtatious conversation when Susan caught Jack's eye. Susan rushed out of the nightclub and took a cab home.

Later, Jack reprimanded Susan for embarrassing him when she left the club. He explained that the woman, a recent college graduate, had asked him about his business. He'd intended to give her career advice but had drunk too much and didn't realize the conversation had gone on so long.

Susan wrestled with her reservations about marrying Jack, but her doubts receded several nights later as she prepared to get into bed. She drew back the bedcovers and found two airplane tickets to Grand Cayman on the sheet, along with Jack's note. In bold letters, he had written, "I love you. You are the only woman I want."

After they married, Jack and Susan got season tickets to sports events, socialized with friends, went away for long weekends, and indulged in lazy Sunday afternoons. Susan saw that their marriage suited Jack. The painful breakup with his first wife seemed to fade into the past, and he appeared content and more affectionate with her. Susan committed to showing him what a great partner she could be.

Jack wanted to be with Susan all the time and discouraged her from visits with her friends and family members. One night at a party, he found her across a crowded room, pulled her aside, and chastised her for not staying beside him. When they arrived home, a heated argument ended when he left the house. Late the next day, Jack came home but declined to talk about the incident for hours. He broke his silence with more blame. "If you really loved me, you wouldn't have been so anxious to fall all over other guys at the party," he complained. "You're just like everyone else who wants to push me to the side until they need me for something. I'm sick and tired of taking care of other people who only think of themselves. No one really cares about me at all."

Although agitated about their scuffle and Jack's disappearance, Susan realized the futility in talking to Jack. He defended himself and made excuses. She stifled her feelings and assumed that his display of jealousy and vulnerability proved how much he loved her.

One evening, as they watched a soccer game on television, Susan got the name of a player wrong. Jack called her a space cadet. When she responded, "I don't appreciate being called a space cadet," he echoed her words in a jeering voice. Susan leaped off the couch and darted out of the room.

Jack followed Susan around the house and heckled her. "Awwwww ... What's wrong wif da wittle baby?" he scoffed.

She screamed at him to go away, but he continued. She hurled an ashtray at him, and she broke down in tears.

Afterward, Susan felt deep sadness and disappointment in herself. She concluded that Jack, understandably, had gotten annoyed with her because he had a higher level of intelligence than she did. If she had a quicker mind, she could meet and match his wits. Susan, who normally drank in moderation, dulled her heartache with a bottle of wine.

The next morning, Jack confirmed Susan's thoughts. "You know your empty-headed comments make me crazy. If you stopped to think before you talked, we could have had a nice evening together." He admonished Susan for her inability to control her temper and her overindulgence in alcohol. Full of remorse and depleted from lack of sleep, Susan disliked herself for her reckless behavior.

On the night of their wedding anniversary, Jack took Susan to a trendy restaurant. At a cozy table for two that Jack prearranged, he slid a blue box from Tiffany's across the table to Susan. She yanked off the ribbon and box top, gasped at the sight of a diamond pendant necklace, and thanked him for his thoughtfulness. "You know I love you," Jack announced right on cue, "but you really get to me sometimes because of the way you act. I hope you finally understand what I'm talking about."

Susan didn't understand what Jack meant when he said "the way you act," but she didn't want to mar their anniversary with a discussion that would cause hard feelings between them. Jack lifted the jewelry out of the box, stood behind Susan, and fastened the necklace around her neck. Susan imagined a noose instead.

At dinner Jack amused Susan with stories about his work and made funny comments about people in the restaurant. Although Susan longed to let herself go and enjoy the evening, her intuition told her to be careful; if she let down her defenses, she might get hurt.

Susan gazed across the table at the man she had chosen to be with for a lifetime. His golden-blond hair brushed against the collar of his navy-blue jacket and crisp white shirt. Tall and fit, with a smile that could melt wax, Jack symbolized the man of her dreams, but all too often he appeared to be more like a character in a nightmare. Susan appreciated Jack's generosity and his sense of fun, but she hungered for a deeper and more fulfilling connection with him, one that honored her needs, feelings, personal interests, and opinions. She seemed to be invisible to Jack, except when he needed her.

Jack's plan for a lovely evening together and his carefully selected gift rekindled Susan's hope that they could be closer as a couple. She looked forward to spending time with him later, beside the fireplace in their bedroom.

After dinner, Jack pulled up in their driveway but stayed in the car. He reminded Susan that he had promised to join work colleagues after dinner to celebrate a lucrative business contract.

Susan swallowed hard and squinted at Jack. "You didn't tell me you were going out after dinner."

Jack countered, "I told you yesterday. You were tuned out, as usual."

Susan stood on the pavement and watched Jack speed off, her head dizzy with thoughts. *I would have remembered if he told me he would be going out after dinner on our anniversary night. Maybe he told me and I wasn't listening. Is he bored with me? Is he telling me the truth? Did he make up an excuse so he could meet another woman?*

When Jack returned at three o'clock in the morning, Susan woke to the smell of alcohol and the chill of Jack's body sidling up to her in bed. Susan's disappointment in Jack still hurt, but she gave in to sex with him to avoid a fight. She knew refusal would provoke an argument, and she wanted to be on speaking terms for a family gathering at her mother's house the next day.

In the morning, Jack woke up moody and distant. Susan poured coffee and watched him knock around the kitchen, banging pots and cabinet doors. Susan asked Jack if she had upset him. "Why don't you stop playing innocent and admit what you did," he grumbled, a clear message to back off. Jack's accusation bewildered Susan, but she kept quiet to avoid a brawl.

At Sunday brunch, Jack exuded charisma. He engaged her family members, who responded to him with great interest. Jack read a story from a children's book to Susan's five-year-old nephew as his mother, Susan's sister, smiled gratefully. Disheartened by Jack's behavior the night before, Susan put on a cheerful front so that no one would suspect her state of mind.

Shifts in Jack's behavior and his mixed messages kept Susan emotionally off balance. She contemplated their relationship. *Who's causing the trouble? Is it him or me?*

Answers to her questions eluded her, however. Jack professed to love her, but his actions didn't support his words. If he loved her, why did he keep a ready list of personal improvements he insisted she make? He would say, "We could be great together if only you would change ..." and follow with a description of her unappealing personality traits, misguided opinions and choices, and annoying habits.

Susan struggled to make sense out of Jack's analysis. "Just what do you love about me?" she queried.

He explained, "You misunderstand me. I'm just trying to help you because I care."

The contradiction of Jack's words and his actions stumped Susan, but she soldiered on to do what she could to restore their relationship.

While dressing to attend a movie with two friends, Jack wrapped his arms around Susan. He stroked her hair and complimented her on her dress. "I'm proud to be with you," he remarked.

After the film, the four friends talked cordially on the way to dinner. "I thought the film illustrated a great example of how capitalism affects democracy," Susan stated.

Jack rolled his eyes and smirked at Susan. "You're very naive and shouldn't comment on matters you know nothing about. Do us all a favor and keep your opinions to yourself."

Susan's pulse accelerated and her palms grew sweaty. She managed an awkward laugh, but she kept quiet the rest of the evening for fear of more demeaning retorts. Jack had warned her to think before she talked.

Susan devised a plan to win Jack's admiration. She subscribed to news magazines, joined a local tennis league, and attended an interior design course. But instead of appreciation, Jack chided her. "You need to stop wasting so much time and money on yourself. Besides, you'll make a fool out of yourself if you try to play competitive tennis."

Crushed by Jack's lack of approval, Susan subsisted on his occasional words of reassurance. When she detected that he might be approachable, she urged him to talk with her about ways they could better their marriage. Jack eschewed conciliatory discussions, though. "It's not the right time," he said.

When Jack *did* talk with Susan, he stepped over her words, refuted her statements, and belittled her intelligence. She couldn't think of what to say when he forced his opinions on her as if her sentiments and viewpoints rang hollow. She berated herself for her lack of confidence.

Susan conducted an exhaustive mental analysis of the reasons for their trouble, but she always came back to the same dark place in her mind. *It's my fault,* she decided. *If I could be smarter, sexier, or more entertaining, he would listen to me. He would love me then.*

As she questioned the quality of her marriage, Susan contemplated her lack of experience in long-term relationships. Friends at work told Susan that committed relationships require hard work. Several of her coworkers told stories about their partners' physical abuse and sexual liaisons with others. Susan took comfort in the absence of such deal breakers in her marriage.

Susan focused on recapturing the romance that had consumed them in the early years, in an effort to reignite Jack's passion. She left love notes for him around the house, bought his favorite foods, and cooked homemade dinners.

After his arrival from work one evening, Jack followed a trail of Susan's clothes from the front door to the bedroom, where she posed alluringly in bed, clad in new lingerie. He slipped into bed and enveloped her in his arms. She whispered into his ear how much she adored and wanted him. Jack pulled at her lingerie, demeaned her with vulgar words, satisfied himself sexually, and left her disturbed and frustrated. She had anticipated tender and passionate lovemaking, but instead he manhandled her.

The occasional good times with Jack prolonged Susan's hope that their relationship would improve.

One Sunday afternoon, Susan came home from an out-of-town business conference. As she approached the house, she noticed a newly landscaped lawn with daylily, salvia, and bearded iris flowers and camellia, hydrangea, and azalea bushes. Jack kissed her and told her he had worked all weekend to surprise her. That evening, they snuggled on the couch and watched a movie. His loving actions resuscitated her warmth toward him. She set her mind to initiate more enjoyable times together.

Seeing an opportunity to repair the cracks in their marriage, Susan found a marital and family therapist and asked Jack to attend therapy with her. He held up his hands and shook his head. "I don't believe in counselors," he groaned. "They are a waste of time and money."

Susan ached for harmony with Jack, but without his involvement, she alone bore the burden of rebuilding their relationship. Like a lab rat that scurries through a maze, she kept hitting dead ends. No matter what direction she chose to reach Jack, she couldn't find her way back to him.

In an effort to pinpoint the obstacles in their relationship, Susan developed a habit of retracing all of her dialogue with Jack, but backtracking only led to more questions with vague answers. *Is there something I do to upset him? Could I change my behavior in some way to prevent a negative outcome? Jack says it's my fault. Could I be the cause of all our problems?* Susan's feelings about herself became a reflection of how poorly Jack treated her.

Susan's self-doubt made her reluctant to reveal her anguish to loved ones, but she confided in her mother. "He's stubborn and doesn't listen to what I say," Susan sobbed. "Sometimes he leaves and doesn't tell me where he's going."

Susan's mother brushed the hair out of Susan's eyes and handed her a tissue. "Does he hit you?" asked her mother.

Susan replied, "No. He's never laid a hand on me in that way."

Her mother assured her, "Well, then, you have to understand that men like to be in control. Jack may be difficult at times, but you know he loves you. You married him, so make it work. Things will improve in time."

Susan grappled for a way to explain her torment, but she knew her descriptions sounded weak and couldn't convey the upheaval in her marriage.

Susan's frustration and self-doubt caused her to consider that her emotional pain might be an overreaction to Jack's behavior. Even her mother found Jack's conduct to be normal.

On the way home from her mother's house, Susan turned down the wrong street and ended up in the parking lot of a dilapidated warehouse. She pounded the steering wheel and burst into tears. "Why can't I figure out what's happening to me?" she cried. "My life is falling apart and I don't know what to do and there's no one to talk to." She sniffled and lowered her voice. "Maybe Jack would be happier with another woman, but if I left him, everyone would blame it on me. I will be a failure." Susan took a deep breath, wiped her tears, and drove home. After her visit with her mother, Susan kept her worries to herself.

Deprived of a loving partner and isolated from her family and friends, Susan endured her predicament with no one to support her or validate her anger, frustration, and sadness. Her bottled-up emotions manifested in gripping anxiety and chronic headaches.

After several years of marriage, Susan developed insomnia, feelings of helplessness, and obsessive thoughts about Jack abandoning her. She lost her passion for entertaining, interior design, and playing tennis, and she fell into a depression that she didn't understand. How could she be dissatisfied when she had everything to live for: a career, a beautiful home, disposable income, and a popular and successful husband who said he loved her?

Susan's life became an epic battle to fix her marriage. The more she struggled, the deeper she sank. Susan didn't realize that she enabled Jack's abuse because she didn't allow her intuition to guide her, and she failed to honor her feelings. She envisioned a life of love and happiness with a wise, loving, and compassionate partner, but instead she fell into the snare of emotional abuse.

Under the guise of loving Susan, Jack cultivated shame, guilt, and self-doubt in her, and created an opportunity for him to control her. If Jack had truly loved Susan, he would have done his part to build mutual trust, respect, and moral support. Instead, his systematic attacks on her self-esteem manipulated her into fulfilling his parasitic needs and desires. With a ready source of sustenance, what motivation did he have to change?

Story Epilogue

Susan's marriage to Jack lasted for seven years. She left him when she realized that her health and well-being would continue to deteriorate if she stayed.

During their divorce, Jack continued his emotional abuse tactics. He maligned her by telling everyone he knew that she was mentally unstable and cheated on him with other men. He and his attorney dragged out the divorce for eighteen months in an attempt to inflict emotional harm on her, drain her finances, and ruin her reputation.

In the end, Susan withstood her divorce battle with the assistance of a caring and shrewd attorney and a therapist with expertise in treating emotional abuse survivors. The divorce court decreed to Susan a reasonable divorce settlement, but Jack withheld financial payments, and Susan incurred further time and expense to force his compliance.

Susan didn't fully grasp her predicament until she read about emotional abuse and got into therapy. Her therapist not only provided vital emotional support during Susan's grueling divorce, but she also helped Susan better understand her marriage to Jack. Susan gained insight into the subconscious reasons for her attraction to Jack. She learned about Jack's abuse tactics and their effects on her. She learned how she contributed to the abuse and what she could have done to stand up to Jack and avoid enabling his abuse. She acquired the skills to draw personal boundaries against abusive people and protect herself. In therapy, Susan moved toward recovery from the gut-wrenching emotional pain caused by her marriage to Jack, and she learned how to avoid repeating the experience in her future relationships.

Susan remained single for several years. One day a friend fixed her up on a blind date, during which she met her second husband. They are devoted companions. They treat each other with reverence and loving kindness.

Jack married again soon after his divorce from Susan. When the woman he married realized his emotional abuse, she left. Jack married and divorced a fourth time. He currently lives with a woman who is addicted to alcohol. She endures his abuse because she believes she has no other place to go.

THE EMOTIONAL ABUSE TACTICS JACK USES ON SUSAN

Ambiguous intent (p.40); ambushing (p.69); boomerang (p.87); but, love (p. 61); cheating (p.120); cloak and daggering (p.42); cobwebbing (p.33); crazy-making (p.71); creating a ruse (p.43); defacing (p.103); double-dealer (p.44); dupie (p.132); featherbedding (p.46); flaklash (p.90); gaslighting (p.49); harnessing (p.116); hoodwinking (p.50); hothead (p.91); indicators (p.36); in the dark (p. 108); isolating (p. 133); Jekyll and Hyde (p.52); limpathy (p.53); making a scene (p.134); mock-eyed (p.72); mocking (p.110); mousetrapping (p.55); objectifying (p.117); other blind (p.111); passive-aggressive (p. 56); pity patter (p.65); refusing treatment (p.112); scamouflage (p.37); scrooging (p.67); sexpletive (p.128); sexploiting (p.129); shifting sands (p.58); sick sense (p.39); simmering (p.94); slash-talk (p.113); steamrolling (p.96); stonewalling (p.77); switchbacking (p.78); symbolic violence (p.98); terms of disparagement (p.79); the use excuse (p.126); tied to the whipping post (p.101); tin ear (p.68); trampling (p.80); twist and pout (p.102); whitewashing (p.84); wing clipper (p.119)

THE EFFECTS ON SUSAN AND HER CONTRIBUTORS

CAD magnet (p.139); catching the flu (p.171); chasing your tail (p.143); deteriorating emotional, mental, and physical health (p.173); edgy vigil (p.148); enabling (p.144); fantasizing (p.166); feeding the dragon (p.145); fictional thinking (p.167); going down with the ship (p.174); hooked on hope (p.175); house of mirrors (p.177); ignoring indicators (p.141); internalizing criticism (p.149); judging a crook by its cover (p.142); masking (p.168); mimicking (p.161); muddled (p.150); muzzled (p.152); self-destructive coping (p.163); shell-shocked (p.155); psychosomatic illness (p.178); staging (p.170); tantalust (p.146); walking on thin ice (p.156); white-flagging (p.147)

CHAPTER TWO

Overview of Emotional Abuse

THE PARADOX OF EMOTIONAL ABUSE

The story of Susan and Jack illustrates the paradox of emotional abuse in intimate relationships. Jack's maneuvers paint a picture of their marriage very different from reality. Susan knows there's trouble, but Jack disables her ability to think clearly. She believes he loves her, but she is in a union where love can't exist.

Jack creates a paradox in the relationship with his contradictory actions toward Susan. Where he promises honesty, love, support, and companionship, instead he delivers deception, callous neglect, degradation, and curveball attacks on her self-worth. Susan adores and trusts a man who simulates loving her while he wreaks havoc on her health and well-being.

Susan is lost because she doesn't see Jack's treatment as abuse. To her, the word *abuse* is unthinkable, but his manipulation of her thoughts, feelings, and behavior for his own gain *is* abuse. In her effort to improve the relationship, she enables Jack and contributes to his abuse.

Granted, *abuse* is a word that's hard to hear. It conjures up images of brutish men with fists that stay at the ready to dole out black eyes and bloody noses, men who end up in the clink. Psychological intimidation, however, *is* violence, except it's aimed at the soul. You don't see the blow coming. It leaves no marks because the cuts and bruises are on the inside. Emotional abuse breaks no bones. It breaks hearts.

After years of emotional battering, abused people fade into their relationships. They may begin to take on the characteristics of Stockholm syndrome, in which the captive person develops a traumatic bond with the aggressor and takes on the same values, so that the aggressor is no longer a threat. Although the abused may not be physically captive in their intimate relationships, they can be psychologically captive, so to speak, because they are bonded or emotionally habituated to their partners.

Susan takes on Jack's values the night they watch the soccer game on television and she behaves in a highly unusual manner. She yells at Jack and throws an ashtray at him after he calls her a space cadet. She gets inebriated on a bottle of wine and wallows in dejection. She takes the mental bat Jack uses to beat her, and she beats herself with it.

A traumatic bond with the abuser also causes the abused person to mistake a temporary lack of abuse for an act of kindness. In Susan's and Jack's relationship, she sees his gifts and compliments and his maintenance and lawn projects as signs of his love, but his actions are only a respite from his oppression. They give her false hope that their relationship will improve. To change for the better, Jack would have to work on undoing years of psychological conditioning that ingrained his abusive thinking and behavior—work that is not likely to happen without intensive and, quite possibly, long-term psychotherapy.

I cannot say this enough: Like a light rain that turns into a torrential flood, emotional abuse between lovers seeps imperceptibly into the relationship and eventually washes away general health and well-being. Those in its path pay a terrible price for failing to see they're in harm's way and need to move to higher ground.

ABOUT THOSE WHO ARE SUSCEPTIBLE TO EMOTIONAL ABUSE

Susceptibility to involvement with an abusive person is caused by a variety of factors that include personal character traits, sense of self, psychological issues, family upbringing, and societal influences. Identifying and exploring the reasons for susceptibility will help break the pattern of involvement with abusive people.

The predisposition to accept abuse often stems from childhood. Children whose parents nourish and validate their emotions develop a sense of security and self-confidence in relationships. Children whose parents discourage or inhibit their natural range of emotions learn their feelings don't count, or, in many cases, the expression of feelings is dangerous. Inability to honor and express one's own sentiments obstructs the development of a healthy sense of self, which is essential for self-defense and successful conflict resolution in relationships.

Family life can be a learning ground that teaches children to accept abuse. Children with controlling or abusive parents become conditioned to tolerate the same unacceptable behaviors from other people. To many of them, abusive behavior is normal. They are accustomed to going against their own values and beliefs to cope with the abuse.

In their adult relationships, some people subconsciously recreate the emotional environment of their childhoods in an effort to resolve painful issues. They may choose mates who seem kind, caring, and attentive, but behind the image, they have abusive character traits, just like a parent.

Other adults were sheltered in childhood by parents who meant well but didn't teach their children about the hazards of unqualified trust. Their children grow up to be adults who can't conceive that someone who appears to be courteous and well-adjusted could exact such pain and suffering on others. An abuser's image easily fools people who trust others too quickly; they see their ideal lover, but they don't look beneath the charming surface.

In many cases, subconsciously choosing to be with an abusive partner is about self-devaluation. People with low self-esteem often accept punishment and disrespect, and transgressors confirm their low opinion of themselves. They have a higher than average tolerance for others' self-serving and objectionable behavior.

Those who are susceptible to abuse may have other emotional and psychological issues that draw them to abusers, such as a personality disorder or a victim mentality. People who don't take responsibility for their own poor choices give up their power to resolve their issues and make positive changes, because they believe others "caused" their problems. Sometimes both partners are abusive to each other.

Many people are enticed by partners who seem to be emotionally and physically strong, an image easily created by abusers. On the other hand, those with a nurturing bent are drawn to mates with psychological issues they believe they can "fix," but they are mistaken.

Still others look for partners they can take care of or rescue. Unwittingly, they may choose partners with deeply rooted issues that show up in emotionally abusive conduct, such as lying, manipulation, or a volatile temperament. The rescuers persist in the idea that their love will be a magical cure to transform their troubled mates into the gentle and loving partners that only exist in the rescuers' imaginations.

Psychological issues are often tenacious and can't be changed easily. Therapy must tackle a lifetime of psychological conditioning. People who abuse others are not likely to change until they acknowledge, accept, and take responsibility for their oppression. Then the hard work begins to root out the cause of the issues, the emotions tied to it, and the dysfunctional thinking that leads them to believe abusing others is okay.

In the same way, those who are susceptible to getting involved with an abusive person bring their own years of psychological conditioning into play. They may not be fully aware of their contributions, largely because they disregard their feelings and intuition. They must realize that they are up against a powerful force and need to trust their inner strengths and resources to wrest themselves free of a no-win predicament.

ABOUT THOSE WHO ABUSE

Behind their attractive facades, abusers suppress low self-esteem, fear, anger, emptiness, despair, and often the expectation of abandonment. Many are unwilling to face the pain of their internal conflicts and to realize the destructive coping methods that conceal those conflicts. They disconnect or numb themselves from the pain of their own feelings, so they are unable to recognize or care about the feelings of others.

The emotional needs of abusers weren't met in their formative years, or they were emotionally damaged in some way, usually by their parents or primary caregivers. They become tormented adults who have a driving need to control others because they are terrified of their own vulnerability.

Abusing others, however, is not something they necessarily plan. Many abusers approach relationships as if they must control their partners by any means to keep their partners from hurting them. Their goal is to dominate, even if it means playing heartless mind games and inflicting pain on others.

Abusers may crave closeness, but they work against themselves to create emotional distance, because fear prevents them from relinquishing a sense of control. In many cases, abusers have a psychological blind spot that prevents them from recognizing the humanity in others. They believe their lovers aren't valid except as those lovers serve the abuser.

Abusive people commonly have deeply rooted emotional issues, suffer from mental illness, or both. They often go undiagnosed, but even with a proper diagnosis they can be highly resistant to treatment.

Abusers may have personality disorders, such as narcissistic personality disorder or borderline personality disorder. These people live in a distorted inner world, where they do not consider the facts about themselves and others. Personality disorders profoundly affect the capacity to have healthy relationships.

Other abusers may be sociopathic and have no conscience about hurting people, or they are sadistic and enjoy inflicting pain on others.

Sometimes abusive people, particularly males, find justification for abuse in traditional macho-man roles and historical customs that perpetuate male-to-female emotional abuse. Popular media images frequently portray women as sex objects and glamorize violence and aggressive behaviors. These influences socialize men to believe that dominance and violence against women is their right.

Regardless of the reasons for emotional abuse, if the abuse is not stopped, it will increase in frequency and intensity until abusers undermine their lovers' mental and emotional equilibrium.

Some may think, "But my lover occasionally shows me love and affection, and we have a wonderful time together when he's in a good mood." Granted, there may be sporadic demonstrations of what seem like love and kindness, which may generate hope that abusive partners will change for the better. Be forewarned, however. Abused people easily fall into the trap of false hope as compared with legitimate hope. False hope results in giving an abusive partner too many untaken chances, which contributes to the abuse. Legitimate hope comes from solid evidence that abusers have accepted responsibility, improved their behavior repeatedly and over time, and shown that they deserve to be trusted again.

Here's what you need to remember about abusive people: You can't change them. They have to be willing to change. The tale of the turtle and scorpion illustrates this truth. The scorpion asks the turtle to ferry him across the lake. The turtle expresses his fear that the scorpion will sting him. The scorpion reassures the turtle that there would be no logic in stinging him, that they would both drown. As they cross the river, the scorpion stings the turtle. "You said there would be no logic in stinging me, so why did you do it?" the turtle asks, while he and the scorpion sink into the lake.

The scorpion responds, "Stinging you has nothing to do with logic. It's just my nature."

Likewise, abusing others is often in the nature of the abuser, even if the results are detrimental to both partners.

SOCIOPATHIC PEOPLE LACK EMPATHY

Emotional batterers can be cold, calculating, and without the capacity for guilt and empathy. Research indicates that the incidence of *sociopathy*—the state of having an impaired conscience—among humans is much more prevalent than previously recognized. These people will lie to you and feel no shame or remorse. They are typically skilled at faking character qualities that they don't have, such as compassion and thoughtfulness.

Sociopathic people show up in all walks of life and professions, including in positions of authority over others (teachers, ministers, physicians, and police officers, to name a few). They may be among your friends or family members. You can't open up and invite intimacy with sociopathic people. Doing so creates opportunities they will exploit for self-gratification. To protect yourself, listen to your intuition, get informed by reading about emotional abuse, and become familiar with the tactics, effects, and contributors described in this book.

Abusers Hide behind an Image

Often emotionally abusive people craft images of themselves that easily fool others. They can be personable and attractive and appear devoted to family. They can play the role of victim, or impress others with empathy that is disingenuous. When they are in private, however, their masks come off. No one would suspect how destructive these image-makers can be.

People on the outside may believe the abused partner causes the friction in the relationship. After all, the abused is the one who is whiny, needy, and depressed.

Abused partners struggle to understand the reason why their mates treat them so poorly when their mates are kind to everyone else. The reason is that emotionally abusive people batter the ones they believe can hurt them the most.

Physical Abuse

Physical abuse takes emotional abuse out of the shadows and exposes it. Abused people may gain relief after a physical attack, because it provides public evidence of their private hell. Some abusers will avoid leaving marks on their mates' bodies to prevent proof of vicious behavior. Other abusers twist reason to justify a violent assault, as if the recipient deserved it. No one "deserves" to be abused, ever, under any circumstance.

Emotional abuse often escalates to physical violence. People who think it's okay to violate others may not stop at psychological abuse. Physical aggression usually starts with symbolic violence against inanimate objects. The transgressor may slam doors, hit walls, throw things, or break items, and move on to physical violence against a person. They may pinch, poke, grab, restrain, slap, punch, choke, rape, use weapons, or in some cases, commit homicide or suicide.

If there is physical violence in your relationship, don't try to figure out why, because it may lead to a futile attempt to fix the problem. You (and your children) are in danger. If you were in the wilderness with a lion about to pounce on you, you wouldn't ask, "Is the lion angry, hungry, or protecting its young?" All you need to know is this: run for your life.

ARE YOU IN AN ABUSIVE RELATIONSHIP?

To determine if you're in an abusive relationship, read through the tactics, effects, and contributors in this book and identify the ones that resonate with you. Consider your mate's words and behaviors, but also attitudes, tone of voice, facial expressions, body language, and inaction. Also, take the quizzes in this book and contemplate your relationship in the context of your answers.

Keep a journal of every significant interaction between the two of you. What happened? How did you react? What did you say? How did your mate react? What did your mate say? Did you approach the situation rationally? Did anger get out of hand? Were you able to resolve the issue, or did you both walk away perturbed with each other? How would you describe your mate's emotions at the conclusion of the incident? How would you describe your emotions at the conclusion?

A common indicator of an abusive relationship is when your mate's actions frequently leave you sad, confused, angry, or down on yourself. Also, if your mate apologizes for bad behavior, the apology means nothing if there is no follow-through.

Strange as it seems, it's sometimes difficult to determine if a relationship is emotionally abusive. Identifying abuse tactics, effects, and contributors, writing down your thoughts, and answering specific questions will help you clarify the quality of your relationship.

If you determine your mate is emotionally abusive, you may feel empathy. He or she was once a child who could have been mistreated by troubled or clueless parents. If you see an abuser as a drowning puppy, however, you may soon find out the puppy is actually a viper who will bite you as you rescue it. You may end up as psychologically damaged as your abusive mate.

The legacy of abuse will likely be passed on to your children unless you stop it. Girls typically learn how to behave in a relationship from their mothers' example, and boys from the way their fathers treat their mothers. Children can follow parental role models regardless of gender, however.

EFFECTS OF ABUSE ON CHILDREN

Emotional abuse in families has powerful and long-term consequences on the children's emotional development. Their daily struggles are similar to those of abused adults, but children are defenseless and don't yet have the mental maturity to cope with abusive caregivers. Children often blame the turmoil on themselves. They are torn between their love for both parents. The hostility they witness and endure corrupts their sense of self-worth and other fundamental aspects of their emotional growth.

Often neither parent—the abuser or the abused—can fulfill their child's needs for healthy emotional development. These children go without much of the nurturing, leadership, and guidance that are vital during their critical years.

Abusers don't see or care about the detrimental effects on the children. Abusers may draw the children into the patterns of abuse, manipulate their perceptions, and use them as pawns to hurt the other parent. Meanwhile, abused parents use most of their emotional, mental, and physical energy to survive their nightmare. As on airplanes when the oxygen masks drop, they must be able to breathe before they can provide oxygen to their children.

Children learn about relationships from their parents' example. Growing up in an abusive environment puts children at higher risk of abusing or being abused as an adult. Parents who accept abuse teach their children that abuse is okay. Parents who stand up to abusers demonstrate that abuse is *not* okay.

PART II

EMOTIONAL ABUSE TACTICS,
EFFECTS, AND CONTRIBUTORS

CHAPTER THREE

Emotional Abuse Tactics

BAIT AND SWITCH: ENSNARING A LOVER

COBWEBBING—Like spiders, cobwebbers spin yarns to catch their prey. They weave fictitious stories about their personal circumstances, character traits, social status, or material possessions to seduce potential mates. They may divulge a troubled background, such as a previous marriage or a criminal record, but they maintain that they were innocent, charged unfairly, or "set up." Potential partners unknowingly encourage cobwebbers to tell more stories when they accept the stories as truth. Cobwebbers can be ordinary liars who lie for personal gain, or pathological liars who often lie for no apparent benefit.

Some cobwebbers live secret lives that they don't reveal to their lovers. They make up excuses for their frequent absences, and sometimes they disappear, never to be seen again. If they stay in their relationships until their duped lovers discover the deceit, they make up more lies to cover up their charades.

Word variations: cobweb, cobwebs, cobwebbed, cobwebber

Joe and Sally work in the same building and have lunched together several times. "I'm not seeing anyone right now," Joe tells Sally.

"My ex-wife broke my heart. I really cared about her, but I couldn't stand her mood swings anymore." Joe goes on to regale Sally with stories about his flights to Washington, DC, in a private jet to attend important events with his high-powered political connections. He adds that he is a major financial contributor to the Boys and Girls Clubs of America and has attended their fundraising events for years.

Sally assumes Joe is honest, and she wants to see more of him. But if Joe were truthful he would tell Sally that he is still married and involved romantically with several other women. He would admit that he spent two years in prison for embezzlement and extortion, and he is currently under investigation for fraud. He would reveal that his only exposure to the Boys and Girls Clubs happened many years ago when he accompanied a former girlfriend to one of the organization's fundraisers.

CROCODILE LOVE—The sentiments abusers have for their "love" objects. Crocodile love is not love. Rather, it's a sense of ownership, something more like a deep, longing sensation for a mate to serve and satisfy the crocodile lover's deviant needs and selfish desires. Crocodile lovers don't respect their mates' feelings, needs, self-esteem, and independence.

Word variation: crocodile lover

Rob tells Annabelle he can't stand to be without her because he loves her so much. He insists they spend all their spare time together. He convinces her that he's never been so in love and "goes crazy" when he thinks about her with another man.

In the first year of their relationship, Annabelle considers Rob her soul mate. She mistakes his intense pursuit as passion and his extreme attentiveness as love. Over time, his "love" constricts her. When she fails to meet his demands or carves out time for herself, he strikes back with frosty silence, punishment, passive-aggressive behavior, or reproachful tirades against her.

In truth, Rob's possessiveness feeds his unhealthy need to deprive Annabelle of her autonomy, so that she will be at his beck and call. In Rob's mind, his needs come first.

INDICATORS (Red Flags)—Warning signs that there's trouble ahead in the relationship. Indicators happen when abusers peek out from behind their polished images to expose undesirable character traits.

Word variation: indicator

Emily gets goose bumps when she's around Richard. He's sexy, bright, and entertaining. They've been together for three months, and she believes they are exclusively with each other. Emily wants to cultivate their relationship, but she is disappointed when he doesn't call her for days at a time and waits until Thursday to see if she has plans for the weekend.

One morning, Richard calls Emily and yells at her. "Where were you last night? You didn't answer your phone. You said you were out with your girlfriends. Are you lying to me?"

Emily is speechless. She can't imagine what she did to make him think she is interested in another man. When she objects to his condemnation, he steps on her words with angry statements and averts reasonable dialogue.

After his jealous fit, Emily is careful to describe in detail where she has been so she won't aggravate his suspicions. She tacitly agrees to tolerate his irrational and controlling rants, which will no doubt increase in frequency if she stays with him.

SCAMOUFLAGE—A scam to seduce a potential partner into believing that the scammer has decent personal values, such as integrity, honesty, and respect for others. Perpetrators camouflage their true characters until their partners commit to a relationship. Gradually, affection, praise, and support become criticism and demands; attentiveness and dependability become distance and lack of reliability. When unsuspecting partners confront perpetrators for changing, perpetrators don't take responsibility for their personal issues. Instead, they blame their partners for changing.

Word variations: scamouflages, scamouflaged, scamouflager, scamouflaging

Bud encourages Sheila's career as a stage actress before they marry. He attends her theatrical productions whether they are local or out of town and showers her with admiration for her acting talents.

After they marry, Bud disapproves of her night performances and whines about her theater tours, but she continues her work as usual. Bud retaliates by blocking her phone calls when she's away so she can't reach him. Sometimes Bud calls her and deliberately upsets her before she goes on stage. He shouts accusations at her and calls her offensive names. One night, she is so disconcerted about Bud that she forgets her lines during a performance.

When she returns home, Sheila has a heart-to-heart talk with Bud. "You knew I was passionate about my career before we married. You signed on willingly to encourage and support my career," Sheila reminds him. "Now you've taken a 180-degree turn. What happened to you?"

Bud won't admit to Sheila that he didn't reveal his true self and went along with her career so she would marry him. Instead he lies. "You misled me about your career," he protests. "If you really loved me, you would put me first."

Sheila is floored. She wonders how Bud could be so unlike the man she thought she married.

SICK SENSE—The ability to zero in on another person's vulnerabilities for personal gain or sadistic pleasure. Like a shark that detects drops of blood in distant water, people who have a sick sense are drawn to those they can deceive and manipulate. They circle closer and closer to victims until they have them in their maws. The sick sensor then cultivates the victim's weaknesses and hurts her or him in ways that inflict the most pain.

Word variations: sick senses, sick sensor

Suzanne is shy and lacks self-confidence. Her greatest fears are rejection and being seen as stupid or inadequate. She grew up in a military family that moved to a different place every year, and to make friends at each new school, she became a people pleaser. Suzanne's shyness makes it difficult for her to be the center of attention, because she gets nervous and can't think of what to say.

When Suzanne meets Tad, he senses her lack of self-confidence and need to please. While they are dating, he shows just enough interest in her to activate her fear of rejection and trigger her need for his acceptance. He alternates between warmth and punishing criticism to manipulate her into staying with him. After they marry, Tad humiliates Suzanne in public, belittles her intelligence, and disrespects her feelings. He fosters her sense of inadequacy by blaming her and refusing to discuss their issues, so he can control her.

DECEPTIVE DEVICES: CREATING CONFUSION

AMBIGUOUS INTENT—The intention that underlies many hidden emotional abuse tactics and a particularly effective way to destabilize a partner. Ambiguous intent involves the use of deception, contradiction, inconsistencies between words and behavior, and conflicting verbal and nonverbal language. Those with ambiguous intentions appear to love and nurture their partners, but their actual intentions are to create self-doubt and confusion for better control.

Word variations: ambiguous intents, ambiguous intentions

When out with friends, Judd tells a story about Marla that knocks her intelligence and embarrasses her. He calls her a dumbo.

After returning home, Marla complains to Judd that his actions were way out of line. Judd gives the impression that he is trying to have a meaningful conversation to resolve the issue, but he hides his intent, which is to plant guilt and uncertainty in her mind.

He puts his arm around her and says, "Don't you realize that I was just kidding? You know I love you more than anyone in the world. I would never want to hurt you."

In an effort to understand him, she asks him to explain why he made her the butt of a joke, but he blocks her objections with the claim that she doesn't listen to him. She finds it difficult to react because his words don't fit his actions, and there's no clarity in what he says.

Marla isn't sure whether or not she overreacted to Judd's comments. The more she tries to comprehend his actions, the more he confuses her with platitudes, denial, and blame. In the end, she is overcome with despair, and the original issue is left unresolved.

Ambiguous Intent

CLOAK AND DAGGERING—When abusers obscure the truth under a cloak of subterfuge and denial, and the effect on the abused is like a dagger to the heart. Those who are cloak and daggered may discount their intuition and take the blame.

Word variations: cloak and daggers, cloak and daggered

Hallie is unhappy in her marriage to Damon, but she can't put her finger on the reason. They don't argue or have loud fights the way her neighbors do. Damon works a lot, and when he's home, he stays by himself. "I love you. There's nothing wrong," he assures her when she urges him to talk about their relationship. Hallie's lack of emotional connection with Damon causes her acute emotional pain, but she's stymied by his refusal to open up. She blames herself for his indifference and believes he is no longer interested in her.

In truth, Damon is overcome with self-loathing and unwilling to work through his fear of emotional intimacy. He secretly uses pornography for sexual gratification and a false sense of intimacy.

CREATING A RUSE—What's an effective way to distract partners from suspecting forbidden behaviors? Create a ruse. Ruse creators pick fights or make accusations against their partners, so they will have an excuse to go away for hours to do whatever they please. Upon the abuser's return, the partner left at home is focused on reconciliation and not where the ruse creator has been.

Word variations: create a ruse, creates a ruse, created a ruse, ruse creator

Matt comes home from work to his wife, Beth Ann, and their two young sons. He glances around the house and upbraids her for what he deems are her substandard domestic skills. "What have you done all day?" He throws up his arms. "The house is a mess. I work hard to support you and the kids, and I can't even get a hot dinner when I get home. What kind of wife are you?"

After he harangues her for another ten minutes, he announces he's off to get his own dinner and stomps out of the house. Matt doesn't come home until after midnight, having spent the evening with another woman.

Beth Ann is relieved that Matt is home and doesn't question him about where he's been. She shopped for groceries and cleaned the house and wants his approval.

DOUBLE-DEALER—People who breach their purported values and beliefs as it serves them, even if it oppresses others. However, they insist that their mates adhere strictly to the same values and beliefs, usually when there is a benefit for the double-dealers.

Word variations: double-dealing, double-deal

When Debbie meets Bill, he works as a Catholic youth minister, reads religious books, and goes to church several times a week. They attend Catholic Mass before dates. Along with Bill's religious sermons, he lectures on the importance of family values. Debbie decides Bill will be an ideal husband and father.

After they marry, Bill and Debbie observe Catholic principles, including the prohibition on contraception. Bill quickly tires of sex only for procreation, however, and insists that Debbie use birth control. Nevertheless, he quits talking to his sister when she and her husband use birth control to plan their family.

At youth ministry retreats, Bill radiates kindness and understanding, and teaches religious doctrine with enthusiasm. At home, however, his menacing presence comes out. He calls Debbie vulgar names, screams false accusations at her, and makes impossible demands on her time. He uses religion to justify his sexual affairs.

When Debbie is seven months pregnant and has an eighteen-month-old child, she sits at her desk and sorts through dozens of precious old family photographs to put in a keepsake album. Bill shouts at her for having a messy desk, stuffs the photos in a trash bag, and puts the bag in a Dumpster. When an argument ensues, he threatens Debbie with a loaded gun.

After the birth of their child, Debbie takes the children, leaves Bill, and files for divorce. Bill posts scripture on social media sites and condemns Debbie. He gathers friends and family members and entreats them to pray with him so Debbie will change her mind.

Debbie succeeds in divorcing Bill. When the children stay with him in the summer, he refuses to take them to Sunday school and spanks the youngest child when the child calls out for his mother in the night.

FEATHERBEDDING—Coming to bed at night as if all is well after an abusive episode. Featherbedders fluff up their attitudes with insincere kindness after being uncaring and insensitive to their partners. When the abused declines to have sex because of hurt and anger, the featherbedder accuses the abused of withholding affection and sex, as if there is no reason for the abused's refusal.

Word variations: featherbed, featherbeds, featherbedded, featherbedder

Tanya throws her cell phone on the bed after she tries for the fifth time to get in touch with Nick. He promised to watch their one-year-old and three-year-old children so she could attend her best friend's baby shower, but he hasn't come home.

When Nick walks in after the baby shower is over, Tanya is livid with him. "Where have you been?" she cries. "You were supposed to be home hours ago so I could go to the shower. How could you do this to me?"

Nick is angry that Tanya objects to his late arrival. "The guys wanted to play another round of golf, and I couldn't leave them without a foursome! Don't be a nag. Just take the present over to your friend's tomorrow. No big deal."

At bedtime, Nick slips under the covers and snuggles up to Tanya, who turns away. "Come on!" Nick exclaims. "There's no reason to be upset. It's your job to take care of the kids, so get over it. You're being ridiculous." Nick runs his hand over her leg, but his advances repel her. She orders him to sleep on the couch, but he balks. He charges her with being cold and unreasonable and with punishing him by refusing sex.

Featherbedding

FORAGING—Like squirrels that gather acorns to store them for winter, foragers collect and save nuggets of information to use against their partners at another time. Foragers may seem sympathetic during the hunt, but their real intention is to bring up the information when they need it to hurt or control their mates.

Word variations: forage, forages, foraged, forager

Dustin comes home on Tuesday upset about an incident at work, but he doesn't want to talk with his partner, Henrietta, about it. She urges him to tell her what happened. "Oh come on. You'll feel better if you get it off your chest."

Dustin knows Henrietta is right, but she has a tendency to use anything she can against him when she's angry. He needs her support and hopes he can confide in her this time. Dustin tells Henrietta that the advertising campaign he and his team developed didn't fly with his client. At the presentation meeting, the client remarked that the team's ideas were superficial and not well researched. Dustin made a half-baked attempt to cover the team's mistakes, and the client got irritated and walked out of the meeting. Henrietta consoles Dustin, and he feels some relief about the incident at work.

On Saturday, Henrietta prefers to go by herself that evening to her client's art gallery opening, for which she is doing the publicity. She warns Dustin not to talk with her client at the opening, because Dustin might make idiotic remarks and cause her to lose the account. Henrietta's comment stings Dustin, and he decides not to go to the opening.

GASLIGHTING—A term coined from the classic 1944 film *Gaslight*, in which a woman's husband deliberately manipulates her reality until she comes to doubt her sanity. In the film's key scene, set in the late 1800s, the husband dims the gaslight and then denies what he did, which makes his wife think there is something wrong with her. Gaslighters distort the truth, and when others are confused, make statements such as, "You're imagining things. You misunderstood me. You're losing your mind."

Word variations: gaslight, gaslights, gaslighter, gaslit

Travis takes his three children to dinner at one restaurant, but tells their mother, Eva, to meet them at a different restaurant. When Eva doesn't show up, the children ask their father when their mother will arrive. "I'm sorry, kids. I don't think your mother cares about us," Travis lies. "She thinks going to the mall is more important."

At home after dinner, Eva asks Travis why he gave her the name of a different restaurant. "I gave you the name of the restaurant where we would be," he responds. "You said you would be there at six o'clock. What's wrong with you? Are you having delusions again?

Eva doubts herself. She thinks, *I've been under such stress lately. Maybe I heard him wrong, or maybe I dreamed that he told me another restaurant. Am I going crazy?*

HOODWINKING—When abusers deceive partners about their actions, desires, or reasons for doing things. The partner's questions or doubts provoke the hoodwinker's hostility and accusations of mistrust.

Word variations: hoodwink, hoodwinks, hoodwinked, hoodwinker

Darren knows his wife, Molly, has $50,000 in her savings account, and he wants control of it. For months, he picks at her to let him invest the money. "Your savings are just sitting in an account. Why don't you let me invest the money? My brother has a great lead on an offshore investment opportunity," he urges her.

Molly has misgivings about handing over her savings to Darren, but he finally persuades her to sign the funds over to him for investment. He assures her that her investment will be safe, and he will monitor it and give her updates. After he makes the investment, he shows her the documents as proof.

Several months later, Darren secretly draws out the money from the investment and transfers it into his bank account. He tells her the offshore government has temporarily seized the investment fund to settle a dispute, but the case will be over soon. Afterward, when Molly asks him for an update on her investment, he berates her for not trusting him.

Two years later, Darren tells her the money is lost, that unknown to him and his brother, the investment fund was fraudulent. He apologizes profusely, acts like the victim, and asks her how he can make it up to her.

Hoodwinking

JEKYLL AND HYDE—Abusive people who live in two worlds, one where they exude charm, warmheartedness, and integrity, and the other where they inflict harm, coldheartedness, and inequity. They come out of hiding in the second world, and their mates bear the brunt of their darker characters.

Word variations: Jekyll and Hydes, Jekyll and Hyding

At a gathering of friends, Jason is the life of the party. He tells funny jokes, hands out compliments, and is respectful to his wife, Ingrid. He brags about her promotion at work, hugs her when the most eyes are on him, and brings her drinks and appetizers.

At home later, Jason launches a verbal attack against Ingrid. "Why did you wear that dress? It makes you look fat and frumpy. You know you embarrassed me when you just sat there on the couch and said nothing. People think you're awfully dull to be with a man like me." He shakes his head and grimaces at her. His eyes widen and he continues. "Did you see Darlene? Now, she's a *real* woman. I think she likes me." Jason threatens to find another woman who will satisfy him if Ingrid doesn't lose weight and wear sexier clothes.

LIMPATHY—The limp substitute for true empathy that abusers use on their partners. Limpathizers are insincere. They want to come across as having an upstanding personal code of ethics, but their actions only serve their own purposes.

Word variations: limpathetic, limpathize, limpathizes, limpathized, limpathizer

Bianca unintentionally gets home an hour late from a business seminar. Santiago waits at the front door. He insults her and charges her with sexual infidelity. He storms into the kitchen, grabs the dinner he brought for her, and throws it on the floor in front of her. "You said you would be home at six o'clock," he shouts. "I picked up dinner and waited for you, but you were out with your boyfriend, no doubt. It's obvious you couldn't care less about me."

Bianca is saddened by Santiago's hostile behavior toward her. She's had a long day and only wanted to get home to rest. Later, Santiago sees that Bianca is upset. He puts his arm around her and tells her he doesn't really think she's been unfaithful. He explains that other men don't give their wives as much freedom as he gives her, and he worries about her when she's out. "My problem is that I'm such a nice guy," he clarifies.

LYING—A handy method of covering up illicit activities such as sex outside a committed relationship, alcohol and drug abuse, gambling, overspending, mendacious financial practices, or criminal deeds. Sooner or later, the method fails to work. Often perpetrators try to cover up their lies with more lies.

Ordinary liars are goal-directed and lie for personal gain or to avoid punishment. The lies of pathological liars don't necessarily have a psychological motive or external benefit. They lie for the sake of lying.

Word variations: lie, lies, lied, liar

Dillon comes home at 4:00 a.m. on Saturday and slips quietly into the guest bedroom. When he gets out of bed at noon, he tells his wife, Abby, that he came in at midnight and slept in the guest room so that he wouldn't wake her. He says he and his assistant worked until 10:00 p.m. to finish a client proposal, and then he dropped by the neighborhood bar to see his bartender friend and have a nightcap. "I needed some time to chill out. It's been a tough week at work to get ready for our meeting on Monday morning," he lies. "I needed to get some real sleep after the stress I've been under."

The truth is Dillon left work at 6:00 p.m., went to the neighborhood bar, and got inebriated. A woman at the bar offered to drive him home, and he ended up at her apartment.

MOUSETRAPPING—To entice a partner's forgiveness with gifts after abusive treatment. It's only a matter of time before the trap snaps shut, and the mousetrapper resumes the abuse.

Word variations: mousetrap, mousetraps, mousetrapped, mousetrapper

Marie's parents and younger sister drive from North Carolina to Tennessee to spend Thanksgiving with Marie and her husband, Eddie. Shortly after they arrive, Eddie asks them when they plan to leave. While they visit, Eddie stays by himself most of the time, and when he's around, he is sullen and distant and makes them feel unwelcome. He knows Marie will give in to him while her family is visiting, so he picks fights with her.

Marie struggles to compensate for Eddie's behavior, and she makes excuses for him. When her family leaves, she hugs them good-bye, waves them off with a smile, and collapses onto her bed in disappointment and exhaustion.

Several days later, Marie notices a white velvet box on her dresser. Inside, there is a pair of David Yurman drop earrings with garnets and diamonds. Marie is exasperated with Eddie for the way he treated her family, but she puts her grievances aside. She convinces herself that the earrings are Eddie's way to apologize, and hopes his behavior improves.

PASSIVE-AGGRESSIVE—A pattern of behavior that is an indirect expression of hostility towards a partner. The passive-aggressor uses devious actions to hide an intent to frustrate, distress, hurt, or punish a partner. Behaviors include procrastination, resistance, stubbornness, forgetfulness, sullenness, and demeaning jokes. Passive-aggressors may seem agreeable, but they do not follow through on their promises, statements, or commitments. They make empty excuses or apologies for their actions or turn the blame for the trouble on their innocent partners.

Word variations: passive-aggression, passive-aggressor

Aaron plans a dinner party at home and promises his wife, Alice, he will do all the required work. The afternoon before the party, Aaron leaves the house and returns too late to prepare for their guests.

Alice arrives home from work and sees that Aaron has not cleaned, shopped, or cooked. She hurriedly plans a menu, runs to the store for groceries, bakes fish, roasts vegetables, sets out bread, dessert, and drinks, gets all the serving pieces out, and sets the table. In twenty minutes, she straightens up the house and changes her clothes.

Alice is exhausted and on edge when Aaron walks in just before the guests arrive. Although she is infuriated with Aaron, she waits to confront him until after the guests depart. "What were you thinking? Do you realize how much work is involved in having people for dinner?" she exclaims.

Aaron crinkles his forehead so he will look concerned. "I meant to get back earlier to get things done, but I lost track of the time. I knew you could handle it."

Alice is so upset with Aaron that she can't sleep. She tosses and turns in bed until three o'clock in the morning.

REVERSING—When transgressors invert the blame for their controlling behavior onto their partners and accuse their partners of being the controlling ones. Reversing frequently causes the accused partners to feel guilt and uncertainty, so they are easier for the abuser to control.

The tactic *reversing* warrants its own term and definition, because it is particularly difficult to identify as an emotional abuse tactic.

Word variations: reverse, reverses, reversed

Andrew uses a variety of methods to control his wife, Sue. He offers to assist her with housework, but doesn't get much done; he commits to doing home maintenance projects, but "forgets" about them; he refuses to help her take care of their infant son; he tells her he will be home at 6:00 p.m., but arrives when it suits him, sometimes after 8:00 p.m.

When Sue objects to his behavior and resists his control, he walks out on her for days. Andrew tells Sue he has no choice but to withdraw from her, because she micromanages him. Sue wrestles with whether or not she is to blame. Later, her desire to avoid controlling Andrew prompts her to stay silent when he goes against her wishes or doesn't honor his promises to her.

SHIFTING SANDS—Contradictory messages and mood shifts that give partners the feeling they are standing on shaky ground. Sand shifters blame their partners for the tremors in their relationships.

Word variations: sand shifter, sand shifting

Hugh seemed easygoing during dinner with his wife, Lucy, and their two children the previous night. In the morning, she wonders why he is irritable. When she asks him if he is annoyed with her, he responds sarcastically, "Of course I am! Why don't you think real hard and figure it out?"

Lucy is perplexed and can't even begin to unravel why Hugh is angry with her, but she is careful to attend to him, so that he will forgive her for whatever she did to upset him.

Later the same day, Hugh is civil to Lucy as she helps him find what he needs to make repairs around the house.

In the evening, they have plans to meet friends for a concert in a nearby park. When they are ready, Hugh bolts out of the house and walks ahead of Lucy to the park. When they meet their friends and find a spot on the lawn to watch the concert, Hugh doesn't offer Lucy the chair he brought and expects her to sit on the ground.

During the concert, Hugh is good-natured and outgoing with their friends, but he treats Lucy as if she is an irritant. As they walk home, Hugh doesn't wait for Lucy and stays several paces ahead of her. His behavior makes her feel sad and awkward. She is torn between whether she should talk with him, or give him space.

When they arrive home, Hugh has a friendly conversation with the babysitter about a football game that his favorite team is winning. He smiles exuberantly at Lucy and asks her if it's okay if he watches the end of the football game with his buddies at a nearby sports bar. He comes home at two o'clock in the morning. The next day, he is courteous to Lucy and acts as though he did nothing wrong.

Shifting Sands

STEALTHING—To sneak around in an effort to acquire information against a partner, such as proof that the partner is dishonest or unfaithful. Those who stealth commonly have illusions about partners, which are caused by their own insecurities. They may install tracking systems or follow partners by other means without their knowledge. Stealthing includes combing through a partner's personal possessions, financial records, computer files, cell phone, social media accounts, or other private domains.

Word variation: stealth

Sam has abandonment issues and is deeply anxious about his relationship with Jake. Jake reassures Sam that he is committed to him and has no interest in another lover. Jake's constant reassurance to Sam, however, doesn't mollify Sam. He drives to Jake's workplace, hides in the parking garage, and spies on Jake as he walks to his car with a coworker to have lunch. Sam later accuses Jake of having sex with the coworker and forbids him to go to lunch with anyone.

Jake is aggravated with Sam for violating his privacy, but he understands Sam's insecurities. He forgives Sam with the stipulation that Sam not spy on him again.

A week later, Jake catches Sam going through Jake's cell phone to search for texts, e-mails, or phone calls to an alleged lover.

STRENGTHENING THE HOLD

BUT, LOVE—The abuser expresses love, but the love is conditional on whether or not the partner makes changes in his or her character traits, even if the changes are unreasonable. The but, lover, however, refuses to make any personal changes for the partner, even if the changes are sensible and important to the relationship.

Word variations: but, lover; but, loving

Jessie takes Joanna out to dinner to celebrate Valentine's Day. As they dine, Jessie tells her he loves her, but to keep his love, she needs to make personal improvements. He itemizes the changes he insists that she make, such as losing weight, exercising every day, never making plans that don't include him, not nagging him to talk with her, and not questioning him when he goes out at night.

Joanna counters Jessie's list with her own list of changes she desires in him, such as to listen to her and honor her feelings, stop criticizing her so much, and tell her where he's going at night. Joanna's list of required changes in Jessie is legitimate and essential to a healthy relationship. Jessie's list of required changes in Joanna is to exert control over her.

ERASING—To take over a partner's household and family responsibilities so that the partner loses a sense of purpose and fulfillment as a spouse and parent.

Word variations: erase, erases

Gary owns a software company, and his wife, Karine, does not work outside the home. She derives satisfaction and pleasure from her role as manager of their household and mother to their ten-year-old and twelve-year-old daughters and sixteen-year-old son. Karine attends school functions and provides her son and daughters with transportation to and from school, sports practice, music lessons, dance lessons, and their friends' homes. She does the housework, cooks the family meals, and attends business and social events with Gary.

One by one, Gary takes away all of Karine's responsibilities. He buys his son a car so the son can do the driving, hires a full-time nanny for the daughters, and employs a housekeeper to keep the house and cook meals. He stops asking Karine to attend functions with him.

Soon Karine has little to do and feels useless. She becomes depressed and questions her identity as a mother and wife. Gary wants the children to see their mother as insignificant so they will see him as the better parent.

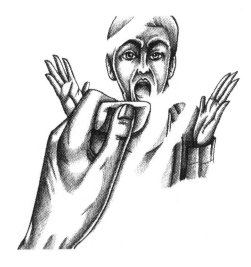

GOING UNDERGROUND—The disappearing act abusers perform when their partners or children want to spend time with them. People go underground for various reasons, such as the inability to face serious personal issues, disbelief that anyone could love them, or a sense of entitlement to do whatever they please, regardless of how it affects their families.

Julian works long hours as a physician, but when he is at home, he stays in his basement hideout, away from his wife, Minnie, and their fourteen-year-old twin daughters. Occasionally, Julian plays basketball with his daughters outside in the driveway, but just long enough to give neighbors the impression that he is a decent father and to feel better about himself as a parent.

When Minnie attempts to get closer to Julian and bring him back into the family, he denies that there are any problems. He justifies time spent alone as necessary to unwind after a stressful day at the hospital.

Julian is so self-absorbed that he doesn't care that his isolation emotionally tears apart his family. His daughters need their father's love and attention as they grow into young women, and his wife is unfulfilled and alone in their marriage. Minnie doesn't understand what's happening, or what to do about it. She blames herself for Julian's apathy.

GUILTING—To foster guilt in a partner for failure to fulfill the guilter's wishes. Guilters seize opportunities to guilt their mates, then refuse to forgive, so their mates feel indebted to them. Guilters often believe their partners are responsible for the guilters' happiness.

Word variations: guilt, guilts, guilted, guilter

Sarah works full-time at an employment agency and has three children. She does what she can to support Jacob during his mother's long-term illness. She cooks and takes dinner over to his mother's house three nights a week, and on weekends, she tidies up her mother-in-law's home and runs errands for her. Sarah is exhausted most nights and unintentionally falls asleep when Jacob keeps her up to talk about his worries.

When Jacob's mother dies, he accuses Sarah of not being there for him throughout his mother's illness. Jacob's criticism makes Sarah feel guilty. She pays special attention to him after the death of his mother, and she hopes he will forgive her. Jacob avoids reasonable discussion to resolve his charges against Sarah, however, so that she will continue to believe she owes him.

PITY PATTER—To justify or defend abusive behavior with claims of victimhood. Abusers attribute their victimhood to enormous stress, too much responsibility, or other hardships. Pity patter may include severe self-criticism or accusations of wrongdoing by others, including the partner. The intention is to manipulate and evoke sympathy and forgiveness. In extreme cases, pity patter may involve threats of suicide or violent actions.

Word variations: pity patters, pity pattered, pity pattering

Joshua comes home from a business trip to an empty house. His wife, Jana, is out to dinner with her parents. When she returns one hour later, Joshua rails against her for not being home to greet him. "If you really cared about me, you would be eager to see me, but your parents are more important to you. You don't love me; no one has ever loved me. My mother never stayed home. I had to fend for myself. I'm sick of always being the one to pick up the slack for others. People just want to use me for their own greedy purposes. Like you—I'm nothing to you but a paycheck," he rants. Joshua gets a gun, loads it, and hands it to Jana. "Go ahead and put a bullet in my head. That's what you really want!"

Jana is frightened by Joshua's violent and senseless tantrum. When she sees an opportunity, she grabs the gun and runs to her car to get away from him.

REELING IN—When abused mates threaten to leave their abusers, the reeling in begins. Abusers plead with their mates to stay. They avow true love and make hollow promises to change their behavior.

Word variations: reel in, reels in, reeled in

Rex can't put up with Zach's abusive treatment any longer. When Rex packs his suitcase and informs Zach he is through with him, Zach pleads with Rex to stay. "Please don't go. I would be lost without you. You're the best thing that's ever happened to me. I promise I will be good to you from now on. All I need is for you to forgive me."

Rex hesitates to believe Zach, because Zach has made the same promises before and not followed through on them, but Rex has second thoughts about leaving Zach. Zach sees Rex faltering on his decision and continues to reel him in. "No relationship is perfect. Just give me one more chance. You won't be sorry. We're going to make it. You'll see."

Rex cares deeply about Zach, and Rex is upset by the prospect of life without him. They share many aspects of their lives, including a social group and common interests, and Rex doesn't want to start over. He puts away his suitcase and gives the relationship another try.

Zach treats Rex well for a couple of weeks until Rex disagrees with Zach. Zach yells and curses at Rex and stays out all night against Rex's wishes.

SCROOGING—To command all or an excessive portion of the family's income, regardless of the effect on the other partner or the family. Scrooges spend money to fulfill their own desires, even when their expenditures jeopardize the family's financial condition.

Word variations: scrooge, scrooges, scrooged

Freddie pressures his wife, Jane, into copurchasing a house that she can't afford. He won't open a joint bank account with her and expects her to pay half their household bills, even though her income is much less than what he earns. Jane is always strapped for cash and rarely has enough money to pay for her personal needs or those of their two daughters.

When Jane asks Freddie to help her with the children's expenses, he gives her only a portion of what she needs and makes her account for every penny. Sometimes he buys their daughters expensive clothing or video games instead of paying for necessary school, sports, and medical expenses.

Meanwhile, Freddie buys the latest communication and media technology for himself and trades in his car every year for a new one. He goes on annual sailing excursions in the Bahamas with his friends. He doesn't save any of his income for contingency funds, investment, retirement, or his children's futures.

TIN EAR—A voluntary disorder that turns abusers' ears into a cold, metallic surface when their partners need to have meaningful discussions with them

Word variation: tin ears

Kate is desperate to talk with David about how unhappy she is in their marriage. He never reveals personal information and doesn't ask about her. She doesn't know how his work is going or what's happening in his life. He has no clue about her needs, feelings, and daily activities. When they transact household or parental business, he is curt to her, as if she is a nuisance to him. He avoids her when they are in the house together, and he sleeps in the guest room. When Kate attempts casual conversation, he cocks his head and raises his hand as if to say, "Don't bother me," or he takes the opportunity to denounce her for her alleged shortcomings.

Sometimes David pretends to listen to Kate, but he distracts her while she's talking by focusing on other activities. She feels emotionally drained at the end of their "discussion." Kate has repeatedly urged David to sit down with her to examine their relationship, but he trots out the same verbal barricade. "It's not a good time to talk."

Kate is preoccupied with finding the precise moment when David might be open to productive discussion. Meanwhile, she is anxious and depressed because she is married to a man who won't hear her.

A Thousand Small Cuts: Targeting Self-Esteem

AMBUSHING—In a seemingly civil conversation, ambushers hurl unexpected insults at their mates to offend or disorient them.

Word variations: ambush, ambushes, ambusher, ambushing

On Christmas Day, partners Sybil and Sasha, Sasha's mother, and other family members exchange gifts and pleasant conversation. The Christmas tree sparkles and glows, stockings hang on the hearth, and everyone is in a festive mood.

Sybil is fond of Sasha's mother and has carefully chosen a sweater for her, but when Sasha's mother puts on the sweater, the size is too small. Sasha contorts her face and shrieks at Sybil, "What a moron! Can't you do anything right? I told you what size she wears."

Sasha's harsh words stun Sybil out of her excitement about giving the gift. Family members within earshot are at a loss for words or pretend they didn't hear Sasha's unkind remark. Sybil tries to soften Sasha's ambush by explaining that she can get the sweater in a larger size. The sweater exchange will be easy, but in the moment, Sasha's reaction humiliates Sybil and darkens the mood.

BLOWING BUBBLES—Making promises to a partner as if the promises are merely bubbles that will soon pop into thin air. Bubble blowers seldom follow through on their commitments, even though they know their lack of action bothers their mates.

Word variations: blow bubbles, blows bubbles, bubble blower, bubble blowing

Calvin frequently promises Keisha that he will help her with household tasks and run errands, but he doesn't honor his promises. He claims to be disorganized and forgetful, but these traits don't affect his personal interests. He never forgets the game times of his favorite basketball and football teams, and he follows through on his responsibilities at work. When Keisha reminds him of his promise to help her, he reprimands her for nagging him. She silently fumes while she carries out the chores herself.

Calvin knows his lack of follow-through exasperates Keisha and creates tension and distance in their relationship, but he continues to break his word. Keisha would be okay with his preference to do less. She's upset because he doesn't care how his actions affect her, and she can't rely on him.

CRAZY-MAKING—To drive a partner into a frenzied state of mind with repetitive displays of unreliability, irresponsibility, hurtfulness, or deceit. Crazy makers deny or downplay the harmful effects of their actions on their partners.

Word variation: crazy maker

When Paula catches John in a lie, he tells another lie to cover up the first one. He ignores her requests to let her know when he won't be home in the evenings or on the weekends, and he allows the kids to stay up late on school nights. Paula likes to keep the house clean and organized, but John disrespects her efforts and tosses food wrappers, bottles, and personal items everywhere. He is vague when Paula checks with him to make sure he pays bills on time. She has expressed her frustration about his lies, thoughtlessness, and bad habits many times, but he won't change.

One night the electricity goes out as Paula is preparing dinner. She loses her composure and screams at John to stop being so negligent. He tells her that she needs to control her temper and not take things so seriously.

MOCK-EYED—The use of eye movements or facial expressions to charge a partner with stupidity or ineptitude. Mock-eyes are usually accompanied by disapproving comments or body gestures. The tactic has maximum effect when performed in public.

Word variations: mock-eye, mock-eyes, mock-eyeing

Myra and Yvette are at an arts and crafts festival, searching for new artwork for their home. Yvette looks at pottery, macramé, watercolors, sculptures, and photographs, but only one painting catches her interest. The oil painting depicts an old red barn and farmhouse in New England that transport Yvette back to her childhood and evoke nostalgic memories. In her mind, she sees herself as a child in the painting, playing with friends at her favorite swimming hole and riding horses through grassy fields.

Yvette finds Myra at another booth and asks her to look at the painting. When Myra and Yvette return to the painting, several people are standing close by. Myra takes one look at the painting and rolls her eyes in disgust, as if to say Yvette is an idiot and has deplorable taste in art. Myra adds, "That painting is amateurish. I wouldn't have it in my house. I know about art, so I'll make the selections."

NO-SEE-UM—An insect in aquatic or semiaquatic areas that is hard to see, but has a sharp sting. No-see-ums happen in ordinary conversation, when the perpetrator issues a cutting remark so unexpected or out of context that only later does the recipient recognize the comment's ill intent. A no-see-um is subtler than an ambush.

Word variation: no-see-ums

Miguel often gives in to Vicki to avoid disagreements, because she insists on having her way. When Miguel resists her control, she looks for opportunities to punish him covertly, so she can claim to be innocent of ill will against him.

On Monday afternoon, Vicki arrives home and tells Miguel all about her new job: the contemporary decor of the office suite, the characteristics of her coworkers, and the specifics of her work duties. She finishes with a description of her boss. "He is smart, good-looking, and makes a lot of money," Vicki jabbers. "If I were single, he's the kind of man I would go for."

After Miguel thinks more in depth about Vicki's comments, he realizes that her remarks imply her dissatisfaction with Miguel. He is threatened by Vicki's obvious attraction to her new boss and worries that she will hold her relationship with her boss over his head as a way to censure him when he disagrees with her.

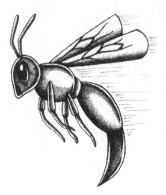

RIDICULUST—The compulsion to commit lengthy attacks of ridicule against a partner to feed a sense of superiority, vent misplaced anger or frustration, or exert control.

Frank castigates Mary throughout their game of tennis. Along with the ball, he lobs insults at her. During pregame practice, he screeches, "What are you doing? You look like a kangaroo trying to play tennis." Even when Mary returns the ball over the net, he tells her she reminds him of a "waddling elephant." Mary hopes that Frank will give her some pointers on her game, but he is too busy with put-downs. She makes an effort to remember the correct way to move so Frank will stop his harsh commentary.

Toward the end of the first game, he shouts at her across the court, "Trying to play tennis with you is like trying to play with a two-year-old child. Jeez, you're such a klutz." In the second game, Frank slams his racket on the ground and announces he is done. Mary leaves the tennis court in tears. She berates herself for her lack of skill at the game.

ROADBLOCKING—When abusers block the road to accountability for their ill-conceived behavior with denial, lies, blame, truth twisting, distortion, and self-righteousness. They are unwilling to admit they are wrong and own their misconduct.

Word variations: roadblock, roadblocks, roadblocked, roadblocker

Laura's partner, Rich, mortifies her at a dinner with her important client. He drinks several martinis and spouts confidential details about Laura's sexual orientation. "Laura couldn't decide if she preferred men or women, but when she met me, we were so good together that she decided she wanted to be with a man," he boasts.

Laura's client shifts in his seat and smiles politely. Laura tries to change the subject, but Rich goes on about her past relationships with women.

On the way home from dinner, Laura voices her hurt and anger with Rich for divulging details about her life that only she has a right to disclose if she chooses, but he denies any wrongdoing. He laughs at her and says she exaggerates his remarks. "You should be happy that I entertained your client at what would have otherwise been a boring dinner. He got a kick out of what I said," Rich states with a sarcastic grin. "You're being silly, so just forget about it. No one really cares about your sex life," he adds, missing her point entirely.

SELECTIVE AMNESIA—The inclination to choose what to remember depending on what self-centered purpose it serves. Those with selective amnesia recall what's important to them and forget what they consider trivial, regardless of how it affects others.

Word variation: selective amnesiac

Leah mentions to Clifford that she wants to see a popular play at the City Theater in two weeks and asks him if he will pick up tickets on his way home from work. "Sure, no problem," he promises. "I go right by the theater."

Leah anticipates a fun evening and makes reservations for a pretheater dinner at one of their favorite restaurants. She reads reviews and discusses the play with friends, who highly recommend it.

The night before the play, Leah selects what she wants to wear and asks Clifford if he needs her to pick up his dry cleaning for their evening out. "What are you talking about?" Clifford responds. "I told you my brother and I are going to a Braves game tomorrow night."

Leah is crestfallen. She scrambles to find tickets to the play, but the show is sold out. She cancels their dinner reservations and sits home and stews while Clifford attends the Atlanta Braves baseball game with his brother.

STONEWALLING—To use prolonged periods of silence and withdrawal to express hostility indirectly, shirk the blame, punish a partner for alleged transgressions, or pressure a partner to be more agreeable.

Word variations: stonewall, stonewalls, stonewalled, stonewaller

Ken expects Ling to do all the housework and take care of their two small children, even though she holds a full-time job. After a stressful day at work, Ling tells Ken she is bushed and needs his assistance with dinner and the laundry. Ken waves her away, pours a glass of wine for himself, and goes into the music room to practice his guitar.

Later that evening, after Ling has cooked, washed the dishes, completed two loads of laundry, and put the children to bed, she asks Ken to help her devise a plan to run the house and take care of the children that works for both of them. He argues that his job is more demanding than her job, so the household and kids are her responsibility alone. When Ling objects to his opinion, Ken walks out of the room and stonewalls her.

Ken leaves Ling with two choices. She can either exhaust herself to keep her job and take care of all the housework and parenting, or press Ken to help her and suffer from his stony silence. Her third choice is to stand up to him, issue an ultimatum, and follow through on it.

SWITCHBACKING—To reverse directions when extending good turns to a partner. Switchbackers offer favors to their partners and retract the favors when they arbitrarily decide their partners don't deserve kindness.

Word variations: switchback, switches back, switched back, switchbackers

Lyle offers to take his two-year-old and four-year-old daughters to a birthday party on Saturday, so that their mother, Margaret, can see a childhood friend who has a three-hour layover at the airport. "You've behaved yourself all week, so I'll give you a break," he states, as if he is her boss.

Margaret works tirelessly to take care of her family, run the household, and keep her job as a blogger for a cooking website. She rarely has a day off and looks forward to an afternoon with her old friend. In anticipation of their visit, Margaret pulls out photo albums to share and reminisces about their childhood days together.

On Saturday morning, Margaret finishes up an article for her weekly blog, grabs her handbag, and walks toward the front door, but Lyle intercepts her. "You forgot to do my laundry, so I don't have anything to wear. You'll have to take the kids to the party. You can meet your friend some other time," he comments casually.

TERMS OF DISPARAGEMENT—The hurtful names abusers call their partners and attempt to disguise as meaningless jokes. The terms attack the partner's abilities, intelligence, physical appearance, or personality traits.

George turns on Natasha's seat warmer in the car on a cold night. After a few minutes, he remarks that he can smell the bacon cooking, which implies that she is overweight and her bottom is the bacon. A few minutes later, George turns his barb into a term of disparagement by referring to Natasha as a "bag o' bacon."

Natasha didn't like his first remark, but she only frowned at him. She realizes she has to stop him or he will continue to refer to her as a bag o' bacon. "Stop calling me a bag o' bacon. I don't like it when you put me down like that," Natasha protests. "Why would you say such a thing?"

George gawks at her in mock surprise. "You know, I'm only kidding," he replies. "You're supposed to laugh, but I guess your fragile ego can't handle a simple joke."

Natasha wonders if she should disregard George's gibes or retaliate with an equally bruising jab, but that is not the way she wants to relate to her partner.

TRAMPLING—When abusers use their voices to squash their partners' attempts to express themselves. Tramplers punctuate conversations with frequent interruptions and defensive or accusatory language to suppress a partner's thoughts, opinions, or feelings. Trampling enables an abuser to dodge responsibility for misconduct and pin the blame on a partner, because trampling prevents the partner from explanations or stating the truth. Trampling may include a harsh tone of voice or aggressive body language.

Word variations: trample, tramples, trampled, trampler

It's six o'clock on Sunday evening, and Theresa is furious with Matthew. He promised to take their five-year-old daughter and seven-year old son to the latest Walt Disney animated film at two o'clock, but he left the house early and hasn't come home. The children are dressed and waiting for their father. "When will Daddy be home?" they ask throughout the day. Theresa tries to mollify the children, but she has not been able to get in touch with Matthew and doesn't know when he plans to get home. She is tied up with preparation for a client meeting early the next morning and can't take them to the movie herself.

Matthew returns home after the children have been put to bed. "Where have you been all day?" Theresa exclaims. "The children are deeply disappointed that …"

Matthew interrupts. "That's just too bad. I had some more important things on my mind. You have no idea how hard I work to take care of you and the children," he huffs.

Theresa tries to make her point, "But you promised them and they've …"

Matthew counters, "You've been home all day. Why didn't you take them to the movie?" Before Theresa can answer, he tramples her again. "I can't do everything. You're in charge of the children. You should see that I'm busy with other things and cover for me."

Matthew continues to talk over Theresa's words with defensive and accusatory language and thwarts any discussion about his failure to fulfill his promise to her and their children.

TWISTING—What abusers do when they don't want to take responsibility for ruthless conduct, poor decisions, or something that didn't turn out well. They spin the truth and twist the blame onto their partners.

Word variations: twist, twists, twisted, twister

In Rachel's sixth month of pregnancy, Brian brings home a large and dangerous guard dog that he formerly used to secure a warehouse where he stores construction equipment for his business. When Rachel protests, Brian tells her that the dog will stay in their fenced-in backyard and won't hurt anyone. He instructs Rachel to feed the dog by opening the sliding glass door and putting the dog's food on the patio.

One rainy day when Brian is out of town, Rachel opens the sliding glass door to put out a bowl of dog food, and the dog muscles his way into the house. Pregnant and alone in the house with a muddy attack dog, Rachel is terrified. She calls the city pound, and they come to the house and capture the dog.

When Brian returns home, he chastises Rachel. "You didn't have to call the pound. The dog wouldn't have hurt you. Besides, you should have been more careful and not let him get in. This is all your fault," he states. Brian retrieves the dog, and several weeks later, the dog bites his mother in the face.

WARPING—The deliberate distortion of a partner's actions, statements, or experience to make the partner sound absurd

Word variations: warp, warps, warped

Julia answers the doorbell on Saturday morning and is surprised to see her brother-in-law at the door. He asks Julia if her husband, Fred, is ready to go to the lake with him and his family for the weekend. He expresses his regret that she is unable to go with them.

Julia is dumbfounded. "Why would you make plans without me?" she asks Fred. "You know I like trips to the lake."

Fred disagrees. "You told me that you don't like being around water," he recalls. "You said you can't stand being in the sun and get seasick in a boat. So I didn't bother asking you to go with us."

Julia remembers that she told Fred she doesn't like to expose her freckled skin to direct sun, but she never told him that she didn't like outings on the lake. Fred's comments have their intended effect on Julia. She is embarrassed by his misrepresentation of her statement, but conflicted about whether he intentionally scrambled her words to prickle her. Julia rushes to get ready to go to the lake and feels sheepish the entire weekend.

WHITEWASHING—The attempt to paint over personal wrongdoing or heartless actions toward a mate by claiming the mate overreacted or exaggerated the whitewasher's behavior.

Word variations: whitewash, whitewashes, whitewashed, whitewasher

Abigail returns from the hair salon proud of her new hairstyle. She had her stylist cut her hair shorter in a trendier fashion. Her new style makes her feel younger and more attractive, and she expects her husband, Dirk, to like it too. She walks into the room where he sits with the newspaper, but he doesn't bother to say hello. She parades through the room to get his attention. He finally looks up, squints at her, and returns to reading. "Did you get your hair thinned?" he utters.

Abigail's face falls and she runs her hand over her hair. Dirk may as well have thrown a glass of cold water in her face. She responds, "Wouldn't it have been just as easy to say something nice?"

Dirk whitewashes his spiteful remark. "You take things too seriously," he maintains. "You need to lighten up."

Using Anger, Intimidation, and Violence as Tools for Abuse

AMPING UP—Mounting anger that leads to hostility against a mate or another target. Amping up usually begins with grumbling and the harsh handling of objects, and it progresses to aggression, which may include acts of violence.

Word variations: amp up, amps up, amped up

Elizabeth wants to hang a large, wood-framed mirror in the dining room, and Warren grudgingly agrees to assist her. Warren holds the tape measure as Elizabeth marks the positions on the wall where she will drill in the anchors to hold the mirror. After a minute, Warren allows the tape measure to snap back into its container. "Hurry up. I don't have all day for this," he moans.

Elizabeth tells him she will need him for a few more minutes, because she wants to make sure the mirror hangs straight and is secured on the wall. Elizabeth finishes her marks and asks Warren to wait until she can get the power drill from the utility room, but while she's gone, he disappears. When she returns with the drill, she calls him, but he doesn't answer.

After she drills the holes and inserts the anchors, Elizabeth finds Warren. He resentfully returns to the dining room to help her hoist the heavy mirror onto the hooks. When they discover that one of the hooks is damaged and must be replaced, Warren loses his temper. He kicks the wall, accuses her of being incompetent, and stomps off. Elizabeth assesses the half-finished job and knows it will sit until she finds a friend to help. She laments that Warren's temper has hindered her project and ruined her day.

BLINDSIDING—An explosive verbal assault in the middle of a cordial conversation that catches the target off guard. The effect on the recipient is like a body blow.

Word variations: blindside, blindsides, blindsided, blindsider

In the car with a small group of friends engaged in amiable conversation, Victor, the driver, swears and yells, "Shut up! I can't drive with all the chatter." His conduct is so sudden and unexpected that the conversation comes to an abrupt halt.

Victor's partner, Kathy, shrinks in her seat and grips the door handle. "I didn't re … uh … realize we got so loud," she offers in an effort to ease the tension. The other three people in the car exchange puzzled expressions, but stay quiet as Victor drives home. They are afraid that more talk may annoy him.

Later, Kathy is hesitant to talk to Victor about his conduct because she knows he will be defensive. The next time they are with friends, Kathy is nervous and preoccupied with the likelihood of another one of Victor's flare-ups.

BOOMERANG—Variable moods that circle around swiftly. Boomerang moods vacillate between warmth and anger, calm and volatility, attention and icy withdrawal, or affection and contempt.

Word variations: boomerangs, boomeranged

William gives Mary Ann the silent treatment all afternoon, and she worries that he'll cancel their plans for dinner and a concert that evening. An hour before their dinner reservation, William gets dressed and is courteous to Mary Ann. During dinner at their favorite restaurant, they enjoy agreeable conversation. Afterward, they hold hands during a portion of the concert, until he shushes her and lets go of her hand for whispering a favorable comment in his ear about the performance.

On the way home, William snidely disagrees with Mary Ann's commentary. "I thought the first violin was brilliant," Mary Ann says. "She played with such passion."

William retorts, "You've got to be kidding. She was the worst violinist I've ever heard. You're showing your ignorance."

Later that night, William snakes his arm around Mary Ann and asks her to wait for him in bed while he goes into the kitchen to get a snack. She hears him rumbling around in the kitchen. A few minutes later, he tromps up the stairs to the bedroom and shouts obscenities at her because he can't find what he wants to eat.

BROODING—Lengthy periods of simmering anger, irritability, or negative talk that dampen a partner's spirits. Brooders don't consider how their antagonistic attitude affects their partners. As compared with appropriate and productive commentary, brooding is self-indulgent and serves no purpose. Brooding behavior worsens when the partner makes any move to cheer up the brooder.

Word variations: brood, broods, brooded, brooder

While Daniel and Dexter are on an ocean cruise to celebrate their fifth anniversary together, Daniel goes overboard with his criticism. He complains that the food is second rate, the excursions are too expensive, the ship's wait staff is too friendly, and the entertainment is dismal.

Dexter attempts to appease Daniel by seeing the humor in his remarks. "At least they're consistent," he jokes. But Daniel wallows in his dark mood and won't be consoled. When Dexter gently places his hand on Daniel's shoulder and encourages him to enjoy himself instead of finding fault, Daniel glares at him. "Stop being such a chump," Daniel gripes. "We paid a lot of money for this cruise and we're getting screwed."

Daniel trudges off and disappears for hours. Dexter is greatly disappointed in Daniel for nitpicking the cruise and spoiling what Dexter hoped would be a special time for them.

COUNTERFITTING—If throwing an angry fit worked the first time, why not try it again? Counterfitting happens when abusers use hostility to get their way, and do it again to avoid responsibility for their aggression.

Word variations: counterfit, counterfits, counterfitted

Mike comes home from work in a cantankerous mood. He walks into the family room and roars at his three young children. He calls them stupid and lazy for watching television, and pitches their toys across the room. Scared, the children run into their bedrooms.

His wife, Greta, comes out of the kitchen, where she has been preparing dinner. She arranges pillows on the couch and motions for him to sit down. She says in a docile voice, "I can see that you're stressed out from work today. Just get comfortable, and I'll bring you a drink and some food so you can relax." She rubs his shoulders and hands the newspaper to him.

Later, after Greta soothes the children and puts them to bed, she sees that Mike has settled down and calmly makes a suggestion. "I know you had a hard day, but that's no excuse to take it out on the children. You hurt them when you call them names. I think you should talk to them in the morning and tell them you're sorry."

Mike won't accept the blame or Greta's advice, however. Instead, he shouts at her. "Stop telling me what to do. I wouldn't have to yell at them if you did your job. You're a lousy mother who allows her children to be worthless. You're the one who should be sorry."

FLAKLASH—The flak abusers use to lash their partners when they don't meet the abusers' insufferable demands. Flaklashers treat their partners with contempt to punish them or seek revenge.

Word variations: flaklashes, flaklashed, flaklashing, flaklasher

Jamal brings three male companions home for dinner without prior notice to his partner, Tamika. The men plop on the furniture and pop open beers from a six-pack they brought with them.

"Hey, Tamika," Jamal yells. "Cook us some dinner and hurry up. We're hungry. We're going to watch the game."

Tamika comes into the living room, greets Jamal's friends, and declines to make dinner. "Why don't you get takeout?" she suggests. "I'm going to take a hot bath and rest. I've been on my feet all day."

Jamal is not pleased. He demands that Tamika make dinner for them. When she repeats her suggestion to get takeout, he lashes her with degrading names. He marches upstairs to her bedroom closet, pulls her hanging clothes off of the rods, and dumps her shoe racks all over the floor. He comes back downstairs and motions his pals to follow him out the front door. "You don't want to eat the slop she slings anyway. Let's go get some real food."

HOTHEAD—Hotheads use hostility to intimidate their partners into submission, get their way, avoid responsibility, or shirk commitments.

Word variations: hotheads, hotheaded, hotheading

Rebecca just got home from her job, and she still has a lot of work to do to get the family ready for their vacation beginning the next day. She walks outside where her husband, Nathan, plays with their dog and asks him to help her out.

Nathan comes into the house and tells her he's going over to a friend's house and will be back late. When she reminds him of the work he promised to do to get ready for their vacation, he snarls at her to get off his back. He gets in her face and screeches, "If it weren't for me, there would be no vacation. *I* pay for the trip. *You* do everything else."

To keep the peace and not spoil their vacation, Rebecca stays up half the night to do the laundry, pack suitcases for herself, Nathan, and their three kids, load the car, and close up the house. Nathan succeeds in hotheading Rebecca to get out of his promise.

MIDNIGHT RIDER—A midnight rider can be compared to a bogeyman. Both appear at night and startle people out of a deep sleep with vile intentions.

Word variations: midnight rides, midnight rides, midnight riding

At 12:30 a.m., Louis yanks the bedcovers off of Emma. Stunned out of a deep sleep, she bolts upright in bed. "I've been awake for an hour and you haven't even noticed!" he growls. "If you really cared about me, you would be all over me. You say you love me, but it's just talk. You disgust me."

Emma is dazed and can't say much. Louis goes on. "You have plenty of time for everything else but me. I'm tired of being ignored. You better shape up or I'll find another woman to replace you, one who knows and appreciates what she has."

Emma wonders where Louis gets his notions about her. She devotes most of her time to taking care of him, at his insistence. She doesn't know what more she can do to please him other than give herself up completely. She is shaken by his senseless tantrum and can't get back to sleep.

The morning after his tirade, Emma tries to talk with Louis about his behavior and how it affected her. He defends his midnight attack, however, and maintains his accusation of neglect, which has the opposite effect of its intended purpose. She is repelled by his treatment of her and doesn't feel safe with him.

RAGING—Life with a partner who rages is like living at the base of an active volcano, although raging is usually detonated by an inconsequential incident. Raging commonly includes symbolic violence, and it can escalate to physical violence.

Word variations: rage, rages, raged, rage-aholic

Leo sits in front of the television. He hollers at Priscilla, who is in the kitchen, to bring him a bottle of beer. Priscilla is making béarnaise sauce, but she stops what she is doing to comply with his request.

When Leo grasps the bottle of beer, he shouts. "I've told you a million times, I want my beer to be cold!" He flings the beer bottle across the room, spilling its contents on the floor. He stomps into the kitchen, jerks open the refrigerator door, and grabs another beer. He ignores miscellaneous items that fall out from the force and bangs the refrigerator door shut.

Priscilla stays in the living room to give Leo a chance to cool down. When he sits back down on the couch to drink his beer, she scoots into the kitchen and finds that her sauce has burned. Priscilla stays on edge because she never knows when Leo's fiery temper will rupture.

SIMMERING—The harsh handling of objects to express hostility or avoid being held accountable for bad behavior. Those who simmer make aggressive body movements, such as flinging small items, thumping flat surfaces, or slamming drawers. Simmering is usually accompanied by grumbling.

Word variations: simmer, simmers, simmered

Marilyn drinks too much at a neighbor's house and embarrasses her partner, Doris, with inappropriate sexual remarks to others. Doris is discomfited by Marilyn's remarks, but Doris doesn't want to cause a scene, so she waits until they get home to confront Marilyn.

At home, Marilyn rushes into the kitchen to clean and put away the covered dish they brought to the party. Doris follows her into the kitchen and attempts to start a conversation, but Marilyn plunks the casserole dish on the counter and the glass top crashes to the floor. Marilyn picks up the glass top and drops it into the sink. She tosses around flatware, bangs cabinet doors shut, and gripes to herself to discourage Doris from approaching her.

Doris knows that when Marilyn is in one of her "moods," Doris can't have a conversation with her. Doris goes to bed and puts off their talk.

SNIPER—A person with an uncanny knack for sudden and malicious retaliation against a partner for a perceived slight against the sniper or failure to comply with the sniper's demands. Snipers, who are masters of grim surprise, destroy a partner's favorite possessions, such as home furnishings, art objects, clothes, or personal accessories. Snipers also smash personal computers, cell phones, and other technological equipment, or delete private files, erase hard drives, change passwords, and sabotage social media accounts.

Word variation: snipers

After many failed attempts to convince her husband, Mark, to treat her with respect, Virginia loses her temper at him. "You're an egotistical, mean-spirited killjoy who lives to mistreat me. You don't care how your actions affect others, no matter how much pain you inflict. You're a real burden to me. Why don't you just grow up!" she vents.

Virginia stays with a friend over the weekend to give Mark time to contemplate her reproach. She hopes he will agree with her and improve his behavior. Mark ponders Virginia's emotional outpouring, but not in the way she wants him to.

Virginia comes home on Sunday and is thunderstruck when she walks through the family room. Mark has chopped down her beloved crape myrtle trees outside the picture window.

STEAMROLLING—When an abuser uses intimidation to crush a partner's attempt to confront the abuser with cheating or other hurtful behaviors

Word variations: steamroll, steamrolls, steamrolled, steamroller

Edith suspects Jonathan of having an affair with a woman at his health club. He spends more time than usual at the club and goes away on weekends without Edith to attend athletic challenge events.

One afternoon, Edith drops by Jonathan's health club without his knowledge. She watches Jonathan as he heaves a barbell at the bench-press station. The woman in question stands over him. He replaces the barbell on the rack, reaches over, and pinches the woman on the behind. The woman laughs and grabs his hand, and they tussle playfully.

Edith rushes home, distraught over confirmation of his cheating. When Jonathan returns from the gym, Edith confronts him about sleeping with the woman at the gym. Jonathan steamrolls her. "First of all, how dare you spy on me, and then make up stories about what I did?" he yells. "That woman is a friend I've known for years. She's training me for an obstacle race."

Jonathan's onslaught is relentless. He goes on to accuse her of an affair with a man at her office. He interrogates her about what she does so late at the office and where she went on her recent business trip. "I'm the one who should be suspicious of you!" he adds.

Edith can hardly get a word in edgewise. She is knocked flat by his reaction and questions her decision to confront him.

Steamrolling

SYMBOLIC VIOLENCE—When angry words extend to physical force against items or property. Transgressors throw, smash, break, slam, or hit objects, or use aggressive body language to vent their hostility. Symbolic violence may escalate to a physical attack on a person or pet animal.

Stella gets home late from work and rustles up what she can find in the kitchen for dinner while Ted sits on the couch. When she's finished cooking, Stella calls Ted in for dinner. He takes one look at his plate filled with corn, potatoes, and shrimp and barks at her, "Are you deaf? I told you I don't want two starches!"

Ted lifts his plate and pitches it against the wall. The plate shatters and food goes everywhere. Stella freezes and a chill runs up her spine; she imagines that she is the plate Ted shattered. He looks at Stella as if he has a right to react violently. "If you would listen to me, I wouldn't have to throw plates. Maybe now you'll get it," he justifies.

In an effort to placate him and protect herself, Stella apologizes to him for her carelessness.

TERRORIZING—The act of committing terror against a partner, to derive sadistic pleasure from the partner's fear and suffering. Terrorists don't care if they endanger their partners. The thrill of exerting their power and frightening their partners is far more important to them.

Word variations: terrorize, terrorizes, terrorized, terrorist

On their way to a party, Edward drives recklessly along a winding two-lane road. The speedometer reaches eighty-five miles per hour and keeps moving up.

Anna's heart booms against her chest and her throat goes dry. She pleads with him to slow down and drive responsibly, but he silences her. "Shut up! I know how to drive."

When the speedometer reaches one hundred miles per hour, Anna grips the console with one hand and the door handle with the other hand. She braces her feet against the floor and cries out, "You're going to kill us. Are you crazy?"

Edward slams on the brakes, swerves the car, and misses an oncoming truck with only seconds to spare. Anna screams and weeps uncontrollably. She entreats him to stop the car and let her out, but Edward punches the accelerator and continues his hellish excursion. He turns his head toward Anna and laughs.

THREATENING SURVIVAL—To undermine a partner's sense of security and survival with emotional or physical violence. Threats may include abandonment, taking away the children, withdrawal of financial support, physical harm, and attacks on religious or spiritual beliefs.

Mindy serves her three young children hot dogs and macaroni at five thirty on a Wednesday afternoon and waits anxiously for her husband, Mack, to arrive home from work. She hears Mack's car pull into the driveway and peeks out the window. When she sees that he has blocked the side of the garage where her car is parked, her pulse rate quickens and she feels faint. She gathers up the children and tells them to go to their room and close the door, that she has to talk with Daddy.

Mindy knows she's in trouble. She had to call Mack at work because the refrigerator broke, and she didn't have the money to get it fixed. She already spent the fifty dollars a week he gives her for groceries.

Mindy braces herself as Mack stomps into the kitchen. "Why did you call me at work today?" he bellows. "I told you never to call me at work."

Mack grabs Mindy's computer from her kitchen desk and smashes it on the floor. He puts her cell phone in his pocket. Mindy is terrified and pleads with Mack to stop his rampage. She has no way to escape or contact anyone for help, which gives Mack free rein to attack her.

Mindy runs into the children's room and finds them hiding in the closet. She hurries them through the house and toward the front door as Mack follows her and shouts threats and obscenities at her. "If you leave the house, don't ever come back, and if you think you're taking the children with you, you're crazy. I'll destroy you!" Mindy picks up their crying fifteen-month-old daughter, but Mack grabs the child out of Mindy's hands. Mindy manages to get through the front door with her other two children and runs to a neighbor's house for safety.

TIED TO THE WHIPPING POST—People tie their partners to the whipping post when they continue to hassle their partners even while their partners attempt to escape. Harassers may beat and kick doors, or corner and restrain their partners.

Word variations: tie to the whipping post, ties to the whipping post, tying to the whipping post

Kerry lost her driver's license when she got caught driving while intoxicated. Michael has been her taxi service for weeks. One night, he gets home from an exhausting day at work, and Kerry asks him to take her to the shopping mall. Michael declines and explains to Kerry that he is tired and wants to rest. He promises to take her to the mall the next day.

"No! I want you to take me now," Kerry objects. Michael relaxes into his favorite chair, but Kerry looms over him and repeats her demand. Michael walks upstairs to get away from her, but she follows him.

"Look, I'm not driving you anywhere tonight, so just back off," Michael asserts. He wanders through the house and hopes that Kerry will settle down, but she continues to shadow him. He slips into the bathroom and locks the door. Kerry beats on the bathroom door and orders him to come out. Soon, her demands turn into a general character assault against him, which she screams through the bathroom door.

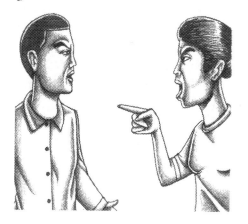

TWIST AND POUT—A method of emotional abuse that involves a two-part tactic. First, perpetrators twist the blame for their abusive behavior onto their mates. Second, they pout for hours to reinforce their claims that their partners deserved the abuse.

Word variations: twists and pouts, twisted and pouted, twisting and pouting

James has been separated from his wife for five years, but they are still legally married. His girlfriend, Blanche, is deeply unhappy that James is still married, even though they have been together for four years. Blanche has told James many times that his marital status distresses her, and that she can't be with him much longer if he continues to stay married, but he refuses to discuss the issue with her.

She gently brings up the subject again on Saturday morning after a pleasant evening together. "I told you I don't want to talk about it. So shut up and stop hassling me!" James growls. "I'll do what I need to do when the time is right." James goes on with his harangue, and Blanche starts to weep. He continues, "You get me so angry I have to defend myself. If you weren't so pigheaded, I wouldn't have to yell at you."

James trudges off and stays in a sanctimonious stupor for hours. Blanche did nothing to trigger his scorn. She only wants to have a meaningful discussion about their relationship.

She finds him in a back room of the house. "James, if you'd only talk with me, we can work this out," she urges him. "I want to feel as though you're committed to me."

James turns his back on her. "Go away. I need some time to get over my anger at you for what you did," he states, implying that Blanche is the abusive one.

INCITING SHAME AND SELF-DOUBT

DEFACING—The public disclosure of sensitive and confidential information about partners to shame them. When the partner confronts the defacer about broken confidences, the defacer slights the partner's reaction. Defacing also includes posting embarrassing photographs, stories, or comments about a partner on social media sites.

Word variations: deface, defaces, defaced, defacer

While they are visiting with friends, Anthony remarks that Josephine would be on the street if it weren't for him. Josephine bristles at Anthony's comment and can't believe that he is so insensitive. Why would he bash her in front of their friends, when they agreed, long ago, for her to be a stay-at-home mom? She is proud to be a mother who is available for her children, but Anthony's dig stirs in her a sense of inadequacy as a partner and insecurity about her dependence on him. She begins to doubt her choice to stay home with the kids.

After the outing, Josephine brings up her concerns to Anthony, but he backpedals. "You took it the wrong way," he retorts. "Everyone knows you're the backbone of our family." In truth, Anthony purposely belittled Josephine, but he's not willing to pay the price for his comment, so he attempts to play down his remark and derail her anger with him.

DOGMATICK—Aggressors who suck the lifeblood out of their partners by using cultural or religious dogma to justify harsh demands and punitive treatment. Dogmaticks adapt their "religion" to serve their own perverse needs and selfish desires. They exploit their partners' religious devotion with prophecies of God's wrath if the partners fail to heed dogmatick rulings.

Word variation: dogmaticks

Walter is a minister who uses scripture for self-aggrandizement. Whenever he wants to control his wife, Eileen, he interprets Bible passages to defend his demands and force her to bend to his will. If she doesn't obey him, he claims she is unfaithful to her religion. Walter warns Eileen that it's "God's will" that man be head of the house and woman should surrender to his domination. He directs her to observe all of his edicts, which include catering to his every need, sex on demand, letting him make all the decisions for both of them, and depositing her monthly paycheck into his account. When Eileen protests, Walter calls her a "bad Christian" and decrees that she will burn in perdition.

DROPPING A STINK BOMB—When their partners are cheerful or involved in amusing activity, stink bombers bring up sore topics, pick a fight, or make an offensive comment to jolt them out of a pleasant mood.

Word variations: stink bomb, stink bombs, stink bombed, stink bombing, stink bomber

Caroline watches Alexander relish a bowl of homemade pasta with sausage and tomatoes and a side of fresh garlic bread during their stay at a picturesque seaside village in Italy. As he digs into his meal, she digs into him. "Do you realize how many calories and how much cholesterol is in that food?" she huffs. "Your waist is starting to spread ... I don't want a fat husband. You should eat a big salad instead."

Alexander reminds Caroline that they are on vacation and politely asks her to allow him to dine in peace, but she continues to harp on him. "Why are you blowing your diet now? Your lack of willpower is pathetic."

Alexander pushes the bread away and looks like he has indigestion, but not from the food. "Will you lay off of me? I'm trying to enjoy my dinner," he protests.

Caroline is silent for a few minutes, then rationalizes her stink bomb. "You know I'm only watching out for you." Alexander raises his hands and calls a truce. He breathes a heavy sigh and motions to the waiter to clear his unfinished plate of food. Caroline's stink bomb has ruined Alexander's enjoyment.

EXPLOITING—The perfect storm brews when one partner has a need to please others to garner acceptance and approval, and the other partner has a need to exploit others for personal gain.

Word variations: exploit, exploits, exploited, exploiter

Christy had a domineering father and a submissive mother. She developed low self-esteem as a result of her father's harsh criticism and her mother's inability to protect her and provide her with emotional support. She learned from a young age that expressing her opinions and feelings could be dangerous. As an adult, she looks to others to validate her and often goes along with people so they will like her, even if they don't have her best interest in mind.

In the first year of her relationship with Peter, he takes advantage of her need to please by gradually asking more of her. Soon, she runs his errands, does most of his housework, and prepares his dinner every night. After they marry, Peter continues to exploit Christy's need for approval, but regardless of how much she does for him, he wants more. She fears he will retaliate, or worse, divorce her if she doesn't fulfill his expectations. The last time she failed to do his banking, he went on for days about how she screwed up his bank account.

Christy is entangled in a never-ending quest to obtain Peter's elusive approval, but he will never cease to use her for his own purposes until she refuses to be his lackey.

HOVERING—Like helicopters, people who hover over their mates buzz around, make loud sounds, and cast dark shadows. Hoverers follow in their mates' tracks to scrutinize and quibble about their activities, decisions, or way of doing things, usually to imply incompetence. The hoverer may redo what the partner has done to emphasize the partner's ineptitude.

Word variations: hover, hovers, hovered, hoverer

Amber rearranges the furniture in the children's playroom to give them more space to move around. When she finishes, her husband, Ron, sees the new arrangement and objects to it. "No, that's all wrong!" he exclaims. "The sofa should go on the opposite wall, and the chairs are too close to the windows." He moves the furniture back into the old position.

The next day, Amber slices her homemade cinnamon raisin bread and fixes peanut butter and jelly sandwiches for the kid's school lunches. Ron comes into the kitchen. "What are you doing? They need something more nutritious than peanut butter and jelly," he carps. He removes the sandwiches from the lunch boxes and makes ham and cheese sandwiches on white bread for the kid's lunches.

Later, Amber folds towels and puts them in the bathroom. Ron doesn't like the way she folds the towels, so he snatches and refolds them.

Amber is dejected by Ron's constant scrutiny. She becomes reluctant to do anything without his opinion.

107

IN THE DARK—What's worse than an angry, moody, or withdrawn partner? No clues about the reasons why. Abusers keep their partners in the dark to undermine their emotional stability, hide illicit activities, or gain a sense of moral or intellectual superiority. Relationship issues aren't revealed, discussed, or resolved.

Rose wakes up early on a Saturday morning and notices that her husband, Alberto, is not in bed. She gets up and walks around the house to look for him, but he is not at home.

Throughout the day, Rose calls him on his cell phone, but she can't reach him. Late in the evening, Alberto returns and tells her he wants to be left alone. Rose is perplexed. He seemed to be in a good mood the day before, and she doesn't know what could have happened to change his temperament.

When she finds him in a back room of the house and asks him if she did something to offend him, he sneers at her. "You know what you did." Rose strains herself to remember the events of the past two days and what she could have done to create a problem between them. She asks him to explain, but he gives her a steely look and walks away.

Why is Alberto keeping Rose in the dark? There could be a number of reasons, none of which is likely to be Rose's fault.

MASTER-AT-ARMS—The self-appointed enforcer of rules and regulations in a relationship. Masters-at-arms inflict rough treatment on their partners to inspire their compliance. Enforcers also ensure that their partners follow through on any plans the partners themselves have made.

Word variation: masters-at-arms

On Friday night, Dave asks Demi what time she plans to get up in the morning. Demi says she will get up at seven o'clock to exercise. In the morning at seven o'clock, Dave jostles Demi awake, but she tells him she didn't sleep well and wants to stay in bed another hour. Dave reminds Demi that she planned to work out. When Demi repeats her intention to get more sleep, Dave rips off the down comforter that covers her, pulls her by the leg, and screeches, "You said you wanted to get up at seven o'clock and exercise, so you're going to get up at seven o'clock and exercise!"

Demi is stunned by Dave's reaction and doesn't understand why he finds it so important for her to follow through on an insignificant plan that has no effect on him. She drags herself out of bed, but she is too upset with Dave to exercise.

MOCKING—When abusers dramatize their derisive words to pack more power into their taunts, especially when the partner is distressed.

Word variations: mock, mocks, mocked, mocker

Cindy and Hilda rarely make decisions together, because Cindy usually has to have her own way. When Hilda doesn't agree with Cindy, Cindy pouts, cries, throws a tantrum, wallows in self-pity, or makes threats until Hilda relents to get relief.

Their latest row occurs when Cindy asks Hilda to cancel her visit with her aging parents to accompany Cindy to a business conference in Chicago. Hilda pleads her case with a description of her father's latest round of ill health. "His diabetes is causing circulation problems in his legs again," Hilda explains, visibly upset. "I don't know how much longer he will live. I have to spend as much time with him as I can."

Cindy reacts with rancor. "You poor little girl," she mocks. "You're gonna be an orphan. 'She's fifty years old and she lost her daddy.' Such a tragedy."

OTHER BLIND—A deficiency of the mind's eye that inhibits a person's ability to see or care about how his or her persecution causes emotional pain and suffering for others

The days are fewer and farther between when Nancy gets relief from Adam's controlling behavior. He imposes his opinions on her, interrogates her about where she goes, and brushes off her feelings. He doesn't hesitate to point out what she does wrong.

One afternoon when Adam is away for the day, Nancy decides to create a flowerbed on their lawn. She believes that Adam surely won't have an opinion about the flowers she plants. Nancy carefully selects some of her favorite blossoms and spends the afternoon planting them. When she's finished, she gazes at the lovely flowers and is proud of her work.

Adam gets home and sees the new flowerbed. "Why didn't you check with me before you dug up the lawn?" he asks. "I had planned to plant bushes in that spot." He orders her to dig up all the flowers.

Weakened by his persistent faultfinding, Nancy bursts into tears. "You're being melodramatic," Adam comments. "I have a right to my opinion about what goes in the garden."

111

REFUSING TREATMENT—Those in need of psychotherapy are often the ones who are most against it. Some abusers agree to therapy, but they don't reveal themselves, tell the truth, or accept responsibility for their transgressions. They may appear to take the blame to convince others of their remorse and willingness to change, but secretly they blame others. They resist treatment and sabotage therapy sessions for their ill-conceived purposes, such as to use disclosures to batter their partners outside of sessions. Even therapists can be deceived by the transgressor's charm.

Word variations: refuse treatment, refuses treatment, refused treatment

Marina is at the end of her rope with Sammy. The family is in turmoil because of his abusive behavior. Their marriage is in trouble, their ten-year-old son got suspended from school for aggression toward other students, and their twelve-year-old daughter has become withdrawn and her grades have plummeted.

Marina finds a psychotherapist who leads therapy groups for angry and controlling men and asks Sammy to get into treatment, but Sammy is full of excuses. He tells Marina that he doesn't need therapy, and that therapists "ask a bunch of nosy questions and then expect a fat check." Marina tries to talk Sammy into allowing the children to get therapy, but he maintains that all the kids need is a smack on their behinds.

SLASH-TALK—The lacerating talk perpetrators use to attack, shame, and debase their partners, especially if the partners resist their control

Word variations: slash-talks, slash-talked, slash-talking, slash-talker

Marnie tells her husband, Maxwell, that she would like to apply to graduate school to get an advanced degree in history so she can teach at a community college, but he tells her they can't afford it.

A few weeks later, Maxwell buys a new Jaguar XKR Coupe without her knowledge or consent. When Marnie asks Maxwell why he thinks it's okay to buy a car that is pricier than graduate school, he slash-talks her. "If you weren't so absorbed in yourself, you'd realize the car is for the whole family. You need to stop being a second-rate mother and think about what our family needs. Going back to school is only for you. You've got a husband and kids now and have to learn to think of someone besides yourself."

Marnie is disturbed; she never meant to be selfish. She only wants to know why Maxwell thinks his indulgence in an expensive sports car for a family of four is more important than her opportunity for personal and career growth. He accuses her of the very offense that he has committed.

BLOCKING PERSONAL GROWTH

CRAB BARRELING—Like a crab that pulls down another crab on its way out of a barrel, crab barrelers obstruct their partners from upward movement. Crab barrelers believe their partners' success will diminish their power over them.

Word variations: crab barrel, crab barrels, crab barreled, crab barreler

Janet has been a stay-at-home mom for fifteen years. Now that the children are older, she wants to return to work in the film industry. When a former colleague offers her a job as a production assistant, her husband, Dean, dashes her excitement. "There's no way you can go back to work," he crabs. "Your job is to take care of me, the house, and the kids. I'm not going to change my life because you think you want to go back to your former career. Those days are over."

Janet is demoralized by Dean's words. She knows that her son and daughter are responsible and can get along without her during the day. The job offer is a rare opportunity for her to fulfill her dream. She makes another attempt to talk with Dean, but to no avail. "You think you're hot stuff. If you went to work, you'd get fired within a week," he taunts.

DOWNPLAYING—When it comes to their partners, downplayers subscribe to the old adage, "What goes up must come down." They minimize a partner's special abilities, talents, accomplishments, or career success. Transgressors have petty, self-serving reasons to downplay their partners' achievements. They are jealous, or fear losing their sense of control over their partners.

Word variations: downplay, downplays, downplayed, downplayer

Becky holds a full-time job as an office manager for a distribution company and is a mother to three children. In college, she majored in English literature and wrote poems, short stories, and feature articles for the university newspaper. Everyone told her she had a promising career as a writer. After graduation, however, her marriage to Emery and raising their children distracted her from her love of writing. Now that the children are older, Becky wants to work on reaching her lifelong goal to be a published author.

For the past year, Becky has spent late night and early morning hours writing fiction. When she wins a writing competition for her short story, she searches through the house to find Emery and show him her award. "They probably gave everyone an award," he remarks.

Becky is sad that Emery won't support her love of writing and recognize her hard work and creativity.

HARNESSING—To bridle partners with frequent demands and saddle them with the burden of obedience, sometimes to a state of exhaustion or collapse. Harnessers rein in their partners when their partners want to fulfill their own needs.

Word variations: harness, harnesses, harnessed, harnesser

Painting is one of Kim's great pleasures in life. It gives her a sense of purpose and accomplishment. But since she married Don, she has little time to herself, much less to pursue her individual aspirations. He insists that she spend her free time on what he deems are more important activities, such as household duties, his errands, elaborate dinner parties for his business clients, and going places with him, whether she wants to or not. Kim tells Don she wishes to take a two-hour art class one night a week, but he doesn't want her to be away in the evenings.

When he is on a business trip, Kim goes to the store and buys art supplies. She starts a portrait of her late mother from a photograph, but soon Don returns home and she is forced to put aside her artwork. When he goes out of town again, she has so much to do for him that she doesn't have the time or energy to work on her painting, and the portrait sits unfinished.

OBJECTIFYING—The failure to acknowledge and appreciate others' humanity, such as their emotions, needs, dreams, desires, preferences, opinions, talents, and interests. Objectifiers believe others are worthless, except in ways that serve the objectifier.

Word variations: objectify, objectifies, objectified, objectifier

Jonah grew up in a family of dictatorial males. He learned that women, such as his mother and two sisters, existed to take care of men. The women do all the housework, shop for and prepare all the meals, and raise the children. Some of them also work outside the home. The men expect the women to keep their opinions and feelings to themselves, defer all decisions to the men, and exist in quiet obedience. The women have no time to pursue personal growth or interests.

Jonah goes through a series of relationships with women, but they either tire of servitude to him and leave, or he discards them for failure to live up to his constrictive demands.

When Jonah meets Kit, he is attentive to her and tells her he's not like his father and brothers. After they marry, he gradually reverts to his old ways and expects her to disregard herself to accommodate his needs. Kit has three choices: she can stand up to Jonah and insist that he change; she can be his servant; or she can split and find a partner who is loving, mutually supportive, and embraces her humanity.

PATRONIZING—To treat partners as if they are inferior and not adult peers. Patronizers believe their abilities, opinions, and choices are morally and intellectually superior to those of their partners. Patronizers tell their partners what they should think and feel.

Word variations: patronize, patronizes, patronized, patronizer

Arnold is a corporate executive who spearheads a business deal with an international corporation and wins a sizable financial bonus. His wife, Jennifer, is curious about the details and asks him to describe what happened. "You never tell me about your work," she states. "I'd like to know the whole story, from beginning to end."

Arnold responds, "The deal is too complicated for you to understand, so don't worry your pretty little head about it." He gives her some money and tells her to go shopping.

Jennifer takes the money, but she feels like a foolish child and resents his treatment. She has long given up on Arnold, because she believes that asserting herself will lead to an argument.

After years of tolerating Arnold's condescension and self-importance to avoid turbulence in their marriage, Jennifer also gives up on herself. She discounts her intelligence and natural abilities and lives in an insulated world of material wealth, but one that is short on personal growth and fulfillment. She has allowed Arnold to arrest her individual development with his patronizing treatment.

WING CLIPPER—A person who discourages a partner from reaching greater heights of personal growth. Wing clippers attempt to cage their partners when the partners go after their own sources of joy and fulfillment.

Word variations: wing clipping, clips wings, clipped wings, clipping wings

Cassandra leaps out of bed one morning, full of inspiration. She has been snapping photographs for weeks and finally has time to work on her creative photography in a makeshift basement studio. She jumps into her clothes, gets a cup of coffee, and hurries downstairs to her studio.

While Cassandra is sorting through photographs to get her creative juices flowing, her husband, Ben, calls her name from the top of the basement stairs. She bites her lip, closes the photography application on her computer, and pushes her printed photographs into a desk drawer.

Ben runs down the stairs and sticks his head into her studio. "What are you doing?" he snarls. "You're wasting your time. You're not an artist, so stop pretending that you are." Ben's comments deflate Cassandra's creative mood. She wonders if he is right about her lack of ability as an artist.

Violating Commitment

CHEATING—To have an emotional or sexual affair with someone while in a committed relationship with another person who would not approve

Word variations: cheat, cheats, cheated, cheater

Wayne and Deanna have been married for eight years and have four small children. For several months, Wayne has met Deanna's "friend," Betsy, for sexual trysts. Wayne's late nights at the office and Betsy's standoffishness don't add up for Deanna, and she suspects they are involved with each other.

When Deanna confronts Wayne, he vehemently denies that he is a cheater. He says a major project at work requires him to stay after hours several nights a week. When it's too late to drive home, he sleeps on his office couch. "That's what it takes to keep the job," he alleges. Deanna has tried calling him when he's at the office, but he doesn't answer his phone. "I turn my phone off so I can focus on my work," he lies.

Wayne's story sounds sketchy, but Deanna has no proof of the affair. Consumed with anguish over his infidelity, she develops stomach pains and insomnia. Wayne's affair and cover-up also hurt their children. He isn't home much, and Deanna's state of mind interferes with attending to her children's emotional needs.

From Charm to Harm

DISPUTING THE EVIDENCE—When partners present clear evidence of cheating to their unfaithful mates, the mates lie to contest the evidence, or assume nonchalance to imply their innocence.

Word variations: dispute the evidence, disputes the evidence, disputed the evidence, evidence disputer

Jim goes out to a popular nightclub with friends and doesn't come home until early morning. Later in the day, his live-in partner, Paige, picks up the jacket he wore the night before and finds pink lint all over it. She feels a burning sensation in the pit of her stomach, and she marches downstairs to confront Jim about the pink lint. "How in the world did so much pink lint get on your jacket? Just what were you doing last night?" she exclaims.

Jim is blasé. "I have no idea where the lint came from," he responds, scratching his head for effect. "Anyway, it's no big deal. I left my jacket at the coat check, and they must have hung it next to a woman's angora sweater or something."

Paige wants to believe Jim is faithful to her, so she chooses to believe the mysterious pink lint could have been a fluke … until she finds a pair of women's black lace panties under their bed that don't belong to Paige.

FICTRIPPING—What do partners do when they want to spend weekends with their illicit lovers? They go away on (fictional) business trips or vacations with "friends." Fictrippers concoct true-sounding details to deflect any suspicions, such as complaints about the trip, or disappointment that phone calls will be limited because of back-to-back meetings or recreational activities. When fictrippers get home, they cover their tracks with more fiction.

Word variations: fictrip, fictrips, fictripped, fictripper

Sigrid tells her husband, Jansen, that she has to attend a business conference in Florida, but the only person she plans to confer with is her lover. She informs Jansen that while she's away, communication with him will be restricted due to all-day seminars, dinners, and a sightseeing tour. She tells him that she dreads the tedium of long meetings in windowless banquet rooms, but wishes he could come along because the excursions will be fun. Sigrid assures Jansen that she will miss him and hopes that he will use his time to go to a baseball game with his buddies.

Jansen believes Sigrid and waits faithfully at home. When she returns from her fictrip, she tells Jansen she caught a stomach virus on the return flight and wants to rest, so he won't ask her questions that might be difficult to answer.

SEXCAPADING—To be involved in sexual escapades outside a committed relationship without the partner's agreement or knowledge. Sexcapading includes pornography, sex clubs, or participation in inappropriate sexual situations. Sexcapading often leads to sex with people outside a committed relationship.

Word variations: sexcapade, sexcapades, sexcapader

Mitt tells Rhonda that he needs time alone and sequesters himself in his basement office most evenings. Rhonda is disillusioned with his isolation from her and their children.

One day when Mitt is at work, Rhonda goes into his basement office and discovers on his computer dozens of hard-core, interactive pornography sites. She is aghast and wonders why he seeks sexual gratification outside their relationship. When she confronts him, he plays down his interest in pornography.

Several nights later, she inadvertently startles Mitt in his office and catches him with his pants down and a webcam. The evidence too overwhelming to deny, Mitt contends he would never resort to pornography if Rhonda liked sex. In truth, Rhonda longs to be with Mitt, but she can't get through the emotional barrier he creates between them with his sexcapading.

ADDICTION, OBSESSION, AND SUBSTANCE ABUSE

CRUTCHING—To use being in recovery from one addiction as a crutch to support and justify involvement in other obsessive behaviors, such as gambling or pornography

Word variations: crutch, crutches, crutched

Allison overlooked Heath's alcohol abuse when she married him ten years ago and gave birth to their two children. She has tolerated his lies, alcoholic stupors, relapses from recovery, absence from the family, and financial strain caused by his lost jobs. Heath has been clean and sober for a year, and Allison dares to hope that he will commit to recovery and their lives will improve.

Her optimism is shattered, however, when she discovers Heath's newly acquired addiction. He has taken up gambling and wiped out their savings to pay his debts. When Allison challenges Heath about gambling, he says his debts are insignificant. "It's only temporary," he promises. "I'm going to win big this weekend, and I'll put the money back in our savings." Heath tells Allison she shouldn't be concerned; she should be thankful that he is clean and sober.

LOST IN THE WOODS—The state of being emotionally detached from one's partner and family. People who are lost in the woods lie or make excuses for their emotional and physical absence and deny personal or relationship issues. They may be involved in risky activities, such as substance abuse, pornography, gambling, affairs, or criminal undertakings. When their partners try to help them out of the woods, they often move deeper into the wilderness.

Alex is never available for high-quality time with Pamela or their children. He says he has to work long hours and stays by himself when he's at home. Every night, Alex expects Pamela to feed the children, help them with their homework, and get them to bed. He doles out excuses when Pamela or the kids ask him to attend school events or family functions. He's out two nights a week until three o'clock in the morning and is evasive when Pamela questions him. She has no idea where he goes and what he does when he's not at home or work.

Pamela is alone, frustrated, and unfulfilled in their marriage. She's perturbed with Alex for being away from home so much, but also for being preoccupied when he is with her or their family. After many attempts to talk with him end in failure, Pamela no longer expects him to change. Their relationship continues to deteriorate.

THE USE EXCUSE—To blame substance abuse for reckless behavior. Perpetrators believe they are not responsible for their conduct when they are under the influence of drugs or alcohol, and their partners should forgive them.

Spencer stays out until the wee hours of the morning and smells like a brewery when he comes home. When Shana snubs his sexual advances, he blisters her with obscenities. She kicks him out of the bedroom, but she can't sleep because he turns up the television volume in the guest room across the hallway. Shana gets up to turn down the television volume and finds Spencer passed out on the floor in the living room. She covers him with a blanket and puts a pillow under his head.

Later that morning, Spencer slumps on a kitchen chair and hangs his head. When Shana comes into the kitchen, he gapes at her in mock disbelief. "What happened last night?" he asks in a friendly tone of voice. "They kept pouring wine in my glass. I didn't realize how much I drank. I was out of it."

His rueful comments are intended to evoke Shana's sympathy and forgiveness, but his callous actions are fresh in her mind. She pours a cup of coffee, glares at him, and walks out of the kitchen.

BATTERY AND SEXUAL HUMILIATION

PHYSICAL ABUSE—Violence toward a partner that involves contact intended to cause emotional or bodily harm. The abuse ranges from unwanted touch to brutal assault. Sometimes physical abusers avoid leaving marks on the abused, so there will be no concrete evidence of their attacks.

Word variations: physically abuse, physically abuses, physically abused, physical abuser

Mona asks Harry to clear the table after she's cooked and served dinner. Harry tells her he's tired and goes into the family room to watch television. Mona follows him and repeats her request. "Harry, I really need you to help me tonight. I've got to finish a report for work that's due tomorrow." Harry tells her to shut up and leave him alone.

Mona returns to the kitchen and finishes cleaning. Harry waits for her behind the door and trips her as she walks out of the kitchen. He jumps on top of her and uses the weight of his body to restrain her. "I'm not letting you up until you promise me you'll never insult me by asking me to do your housework. That's your job," he taunts her. Mona cries and begs him to let her go, but he keeps her down until she has no choice but to make the promise.

SEXPLETIVE—Unwanted sexual expletives or vulgar statements to describe a partner's body, sexuality, or sexual activity. Abusers use sexpletives to degrade their partners when they are alone with them or around others. Sexpletives are used in any type of communication, including texting, e-mail, phone, and social media sites.

Word variation: sexpletives

It's Sunday afternoon and Lynette and her boyfriend, Maury, are at a friend's home to watch a football game. They go into the kitchen, where several of Maury's male friends are involved in conversation next to the bar and dinner buffet. When backs are turned, Maury grabs Lynette's breasts and runs his hands over her. "Not now, Maury," Lynette whispers. "This isn't the time or place for that."

Maury drops his hands and says, loud enough for others to hear, "What happened to the slut in my bed last night?"

Two of Maury's male friends laugh at his comment. Lynette's face reddens with embarrassment. She allowed herself to trust and be vulnerable with Maury and is deeply offended by his insensitivity toward her. His comment disgusts her and makes her feel like a sex object.

SEXPLOITING—To coerce or attempt to coerce partners into sex acts that hurt or humiliate them. Sexploiting includes rape, sexual intimidation, sex on demand, forcing a partner to have sex in unwanted positions, and coercing a partner to have sex with others.

Word variations: sexploit, sexploits, sexploited, sexploiter

Ralph badgers Sheena to let him tie her hands to the bedpost when they have sex, but she is reluctant. She is not interested in rough sex, because it would feel demeaning to her. "Oh, come on. Try something different. I'm not going to hurt you. I'll untie you as soon as you want me to," Ralph promises.

Sheena warily agrees to let him tie her hands to the bedpost, as long as he honors his agreement to stop if she doesn't like it.

During sex, Sheena's confinement frightens and upsets her, and the ropes chafe her wrists. She implores Ralph to untie her, but he ignores her pleas until he is sexually satisfied. Afterward, in response to her tears and anger, he tells her that she is prudish and needs to loosen up.

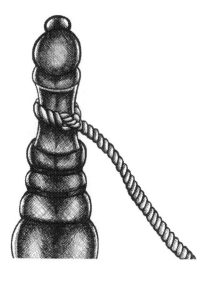

SEXUAL SHAMING—Criticizing a partner's sexuality or sexual ability, loose talk about sexual conquests, or the expression of sexual desire for another person when a partner or others are present. Sexual shaming embarrasses partners and makes them feel inadequate and undesirable. Transgressors also may blame their female partners for getting pregnant.

Word variations: sexually shame, sexually shames, sexually shamed

At a party with friends, Alana notices that her boyfriend, Dominic, is staring at her friend Corinda. When Alana walks over to Dominic and sits beside him, he gushes about Corinda. He says Corinda is "red hot" and he would like to have sex with her. He goes on and on about the way she is dressed, the sexy way she swings her hips when she walks, and her gorgeous smile.

Dominic's careless comments cause Alana to consider that she is sexually deficient and undesirable to him. "I can't believe you would say that," Alana protests. "How do you think that makes me feel?"

Dominic responds, "Oh, don't be so insecure. If I wanted to sleep with her, I would."

Alana wonders if she should be angry with Dominic for his blatant lust for Corinda, or grateful that he has no intention to act on his sexual desire for another woman.

USING OTHER PEOPLE AS TOOLS FOR ABUSE

DRIVING WEDGES—The use of lies or other divisive tactics to cause hard feelings, conflicts, or grudges between partners and their friends, family members, social acquaintances, or work colleagues

Word variations: drive a wedge, drives a wedge, drove a wedge, wedge driver

Shawna confides in her partner, Maddox, her concerns about her close friend Josie. She tells him that Josie is too open with her trust and jumps into bed with men she hardly knows. Shawna says that Josie's fear of being alone causes her to date men who mistreat her. On Saturday, Shawna plans to have a caring but frank discussion with Josie in an effort to help her make better choices. Maddox indicates his support of Shawna's plan to talk with Josie.

Shawna trusts that her conversation with Maddox about Josie will go no further, but Maddox goes out of his way to "bump" into Josie so he can drive a wedge in her friendship with Shawna. He not only breaks Shawna's confidence, but he also twists her words and misrepresents her sentiments about Josie. "Shawna said you've been whoring yourself out to random men lately, because you're desperate for a man and can't help yourself," Maddox says.

Josie is floored by Maddox's remarks and deeply hurt that Shawna talked about her so callously. Maddox's act damages Josie's trust in Shawna and strains their friendship. Josie sends an e-mail message to Shawna canceling their visit on Saturday.

DUPIE—The people abusers recruit to gain allies against their partners and undermine their partners' support from friends, family members, and others. Dupies don't bother to get the facts; they believe the venomous lies abusers tell about their partners. Some dupies are so convinced of the abuser's innocence that they encourage and validate the abuser's ill-conceived actions toward his or her mate.

Word variations: dupies, duped, duping

Martin's mother becomes a dupie when she believes his false claims that his wife, Claire, is moody, selfish, and unable to control her temper. "I try to reason with her," Martin lies, "but she won't listen to me. I'm not sure if I can stay with her." Martin falsely claims that Claire doesn't like his mother and makes fun of her at family events behind her back.

Martin's mother is surprised that the Claire she thought she knew would behave in such a way, but she is sympathetic toward her son when he tells her that Claire causes their marital problems. Martin's mother doesn't know that her son is emotionally abusive to Claire, and that Claire has talked with him about a separation. Martin dupes his mother to prepare her for Claire's possible departure. He wants his mother to believe he is innocent, and Claire is to blame for their breakup.

ISOLATING—When abusers discourage or forbid their partners from spending time with family or friends, so their partners will have no social support system. Isolators want their partners to be dependent on them, because isolators fear abandonment or losing control of their partners. Sometimes isolators will allow their partners to spend time with others, but only if the isolator is present.

Word variations: isolate, isolates, isolated, isolator

Etta's family lives in a distant state, and Etta considers her local friends as her family. When she marries Shane, he dissuades her from visits with her friends. "If you have time to go out to lunch with your friends, you should come have lunch with me," Shane insists. Etta has made plans several times to go out without Shane, but she has had to cancel at the last minute because Shane says he "needs her."

Etta misses her friends and craves their camaraderie, but she believes Shane works hard to support her and their two children, and she is obligated to be accessible to him at his convenience. Meanwhile, Etta's friends have become distant because she is never available. Absent her friendships, her life seems one-dimensional. When Shane is away, she is lonely.

MAKING A SCENE—To create an attention-grabbing scene in public that humiliates partners and forces them into submission

Word variations: scene maker, scene making

Fran and Mick converse quietly as they dine by candlelight at an upscale restaurant. Fran wants to have a meaningful conversation with Mick about their relationship and sees that he's in a lighthearted mood. She takes a chance that he might finally be receptive to her feelings. "Mick, I want to talk about us. It makes me feel bad when you find fault with me so often. I'm getting to the point where I have to think about everything I do or say to make sure it's something you won't criticize. It's making me feel stifled in our relationship. Let's talk about it and find some solutions," she implores.

Mick is so insecure that he views her attempts at productive discussion as an attack on him. "Stop being a horse's ass!" he barks loud enough for others to hear. "Maybe if you'd listen to me, you'd learn something."

People seated nearby stop eating and turn their eyes toward Mick and Fran. She recoils in her chair, looks around the room, and grins self-consciously at onlookers. She takes a sip of wine to steady herself and turns to Mick. "Can we just finish dinner in peace and continue our discussion at home?" she asks.

Mick lowers his voice, but resumes his argument that Fran doesn't listen to him. He knows she is a sitting target when she fears public humiliation.

MALIGNING—The act of spreading malicious gossip about partners to vilify them. The maligner's objective is to convince others of the partner's defective character traits and thereby deflect the blame for relationship problems onto the partner.

Word variations: malign, maligns, maligned, maligner

Jerry maligns Bette when he tells his older sister, Misty, that life with Bette is a daily challenge. "She goes from one extreme to another," Jerry fibs. "She mopes around the house all day and won't talk with me. Then, when I try to help her, she picks a fight and gets hysterical. Other days, she breathes down my neck and tells me what to do. I didn't realize she was a mental case when I married her."

Jerry's false statements influence Misty's opinion of Bette, and Misty feels sorry for her brother. She encourages him to stay at her house when he wants to escape.

The next time Misty sees Bette, she is cold and unfriendly to Bette. In truth, Bette is a fair-minded, energetic, and capable woman. She is depressed and not her natural self because Jerry has chipped away at her self-esteem with his emotional abuse tactics.

PARENTAL ALIENATION—An alienator distances his or her own children from the other parent by using a long-term campaign of lies and derision against that parent. The abuser often builds a team: the abuser and the children against the other parent. An alienator must be seen as the superior parent at all costs. They don't care that their behavior hurts the children, causes them to have life-long psychological issues, and could lead to estrangement from their other parent into adulthood.

Word variation: parental alienator

Ellis treats Susie with contempt, even in front of their six-year-old, Benny, and ten-year-old, Ethan. He faults her for everything that goes wrong, calls her offensive names, and minimizes her pained reactions. He refers to Susie as a "rent-a-mom" who doesn't love the children and only spends time with them when it's convenient for her. Ellis insinuates he is the only one who is qualified to be a parent.

   Ellis's behavior devastates Susie, but it also distresses his two sons. They are confused by their mother's expressions of love and their father's insistence that their mother doesn't love them. The older son is afraid that if he loves his mother, his father won't love him, so the son rebuffs her affection and attention when his father is around.

   One night, Susie sits down beside Ethan, puts her arm around him, and asks if he needs help with his homework. When Ethan looks up and sees his father, he yells at his mother to get away from him. When she doesn't, Ethan punches her in the face.

PAWNING THE CHILDREN—Just as chess pawns have limited strength, but are put on the front lines of battle, an abuser plays his or her own children to hurt the other parent. The abuser tells the children cruel lies, uses them to deliver disdainful messages, and sets the other parent up to look bad in front of the children. A child pawner may also abuse the children in other ways to punish their other parent. Children with parents who pawn them sustain long-term psychological injury.

Word variations: pawn the children, pawns the children, pawned the children, child pawner, child pawning

Maxine is upset with Dwayne for disappearing with another woman at a neighborhood barbecue. At home she takes Dwayne aside and holds him accountable for his conduct. He sneers away her concerns and tells her that the neighbor wanted to show him her new car.

Dwayne walks into the family room, where their four-year-old daughter, Allie, and seven-year-old son, Jimmy, play and he pawns them to hurt Maxine, who stands nearby. He turns to Jimmy. "Mommy is stupid," Dwayne remarks. "Tell her to stop being so stupid." Jimmy looks up, but is puzzled about how to react and says nothing. "Your mother is telling lies again," Dwayne continues. "She makes up crazy stories and expects me to believe them." He orders Jimmy to tell his mother that she is a "big selfish liar." Jimmy doesn't want to hurt his mother, but he fears going against his father.

Dwayne's child pawning not only hurts Maxine; his actions also distress the children. Allie and Jimmy are scared and worried. They don't understand why their father is so mean to their mother.

UNDERMINING PARENTHOOD—A pattern of attempts to persuade the children that their other parent has no authority and shouldn't be taken seriously. The transgressor invalidates the other parent's disciplinary actions, makes important decisions about the children without consulting the other parent, and supports the children's disobedient behavior. The implication is the children should consider the transgressor as their real parent, the one they should respect and obey.

Word variations: undermine parenthood, undermines parenthood, undermined parenthood

Arthur frequently disagrees with Tina's parental decisions, especially when their fourteen-year-old son, Lucas, is within earshot. Tina tries to convince Arthur that they must present a united front for their son's own good, but Arthur won't listen to her. Lucas thinks his father is "cool" and rejects his mother's authority. Lucas won't respond to her requests and goes to his father, who allows Lucas to get his way.

On Saturday afternoon, Arthur takes Lucas to the movies, even though Tina has put him on restriction because he cheated on an exam at school. Arthur tells Lucas that everyone cheats, and the trick is to not get caught. Tina is disheartened about Arthur's lack of support, and she is greatly concerned about Lucas, but without Arthur as an ally, she is perplexed about how to improve the situation.

CHAPTER FOUR

Emotional Abuse Effects and Contributors

ATTRACTION TO A SHINY IMAGE: BLIND TO WHAT LIES BENEATH

CAD MAGNET—A person who chooses lovers who are CADs (controlling, angry, and deceptive) as if they are both magnets drawn to each other, but for different reasons. CAD magnets want intimate companionship, and CADs want lovers they can use and control for their own ill-fated reasons.

A CAD magnet may initially be fooled by the CAD's superficial display of desirable qualities. When the CAD's darker side emerges, a CAD magnet disregards his or her feelings and intuition, excuses the CAD's objectionable behavior, or takes the blame.

Abusers choose CAD magnets for their innate vulnerabilities as well as their positive character traits.

Word variation: CAD magnets

Linda can't understand why she keeps getting involved with difficult men. She never intends to fall for guys who mistreat her, but somehow she ends up in the same kind of relationship every time.

During her childhood, her parents buried thorny issues. They were uncomfortable with confrontation or displays of emotion, and they discouraged the expression of anger, sadness, frustration, or other "unpleasant" emotions. Linda never learned to honor and express her needs and feelings, draw and enforce personal boundaries, or face and resolve problems.

Until Linda gains deeper insight into why she is attracted to controlling men and works on changing her self-sabotaging thinking and behavior, she will continue to choose men who walk all over her.

IGNORING INDICATORS (Red Flags)—People who ignore indicators of potential partners' undesirable character traits are in for a bumpy ride. Indicators provide early and crucial glimpses of future problems in the relationship. Misguided lovers overlook signs of trouble because the signs don't fit the stories they have created about their love interests. As the adage goes, "Love is blind," but there is always an opportunity to take off the blindfold and see the truth.

Lydia and Clint have been together for three months, and she has strong feelings for him. At a bar one night, Clint accuses Lydia of flirting with the man who sits on the bar stool next to her. Clint's voice becomes louder and his complaint escalates into interrogation. He springs from his stool and slams down his glass on the bar. "If you like him so much, then you can be with him tonight," Clint yells as he walks away.

Lydia is flummoxed by his behavior because she only spoke casually to the man at the bar. She hops off her stool and runs after Clint to the parking lot. Clint is already in the car. She jumps into the passenger seat and has barely closed the door when Clint turns on the ignition and punches the gas pedal, spinning the car into the street. Lydia hangs on while she tries to make sense out of Clint's explosive reaction. She believes that he must care deeply for her, because he has been generous with his time and attention to her. She mistakenly concludes that he unintentionally drank too much, and his anger and irrational conduct show how much she means to him.

Clint is an angry and controlling man, however, and his behavior will only get worse, especially if Lydia goes along with it.

JUDGING A CROOK BY ITS COVER—To fall in love with someone who has a deceptive facade. Crooks appear to possess heroic character traits, such as boundless courage, extraordinary success, and impeccable personal values. When the plot thickens, however, dreamy fiction changes to hard fact. The hero disappears, and the unwitting lover stands face-to-face with the antagonist: a domineering, dishonest, and deeply flawed person who causes untold misery.

Gil first meets Courtney at a flashy black-tie dinner to raise funds for a children's charity. From the time he lays his eyes on her, she captivates him. Her raven hair and curvy figure make her look as though she stepped off the cover of a steamy romance novel. She has an Ivy League college degree and owns a thriving public relations agency. Gil is mesmerized by Courtney's go-getter personality and flattered that a woman like her is interested in him. He is happy to go along on the adventure, until there's a major twist in the action.

After Gil and Courtney move in together, he sees behind her glamorous exterior, and the story changes from a fairy tale to a tragedy. She is petty, domineering, dishonest, and has uncontrollable fits of anger. She is driven to succeed at all costs and doesn't care who she crushes in the process.

BEARING THE BURDEN: HOLDING THE RELATIONSHIP TOGETHER

CHASING YOUR TAIL—The unmistakable feeling of going around in circles in an effort to gain the attention and approval of a partner who is ill mannered, moody, indifferent, or seldom available

Connie is distraught by Luke's distance from the family. He rarely spends time with her or their two children. Habitually, he makes promises that he will be home or accompany the family to an event. He breaks his word with excuses, however, often at the last minute, which upsets Connie and the children. In an effort to win him over, Connie runs all his errands, cooks his favorite dinners, and keeps the house orderly and comfortable. She arranges elaborate family outings to show Luke that family life can be fun. Although Luke is scarcely available for Connie, she makes sure that she is always accessible to him when he wants something from her.

Regardless of what she does, however, Luke has a reason for being away from them. Connie is fixated on her idea that if she meets all of Luke's needs and does enough for him, he will become a devoted husband and father, but in truth, she is fostering his behavior by accommodating it.

ENABLING—To accept, tolerate, excuse, or support a mate's abusive behavior in an attempt to cope with the abuse and its harmful effects. Enabling has a self-defeating effect: the more you enable your partner's abuse, the more you *disable* yourself.

Word variations: enable, enables, enabled, enabler

Dorinda grew up with an emotionally abusive mother and is now married to Claude, who treats her just like her mother did. As a little girl, she learned from her father to tolerate abuse. He attempted to lessen the intensity of her mother's wrath by being passive, obedient, and invisible. Dorinda is the same way with Claude and fears that if she makes a wrong move, he will punish her. She never disagrees with him or holds him accountable for his ruthless conduct. She lives for the moments when his need to feel like a nice guy prompts him to be kind to her.

Dorinda accepts Claude's abusive treatment as normal and inescapable. Her parent's marriage is her only role model for intimate relationships. It doesn't occur to her that she has a right to be loved and treated with respect, especially by her partner.

FEEDING THE DRAGON—To have sex with partners to avoid their anger and maltreatment. When dragons are refused, they breathe fire because they believe their partners "owe" them sex, regardless of the quality of the relationship. Dragons use sex for power and dominance and as an attempt to meet all their emotional needs; they have severed any other emotional connection with their partners by abusing them.

Word variations: feed the dragon, fed the dragon, dragon feeder, dragon feeding

It's four o'clock in the afternoon and Carla is cooking a big dinner for a family gathering to be held in her home. Everyone is due to arrive at five o'clock. She rushes around the kitchen so the food, drinks, and table setting will be ready in time.

Her husband, Sean, sees that she is busy, but he has no regard for her time. His need for attention comes first. He grabs her buttocks, spins her around, and pulls her toward him. Carla tells him to stop and explains that she still has a lot to get done before her family arrives. But Sean bothers her until she gives up, turns off the stove, and allows him to lead her into the bedroom.

Carla is repulsed by Sean's demanding, self-absorbed behavior, but she complies with him to avoid a fight. She doesn't want him to be in an irritable mood, but she overlooks her own feelings. She hides her shame for compromising herself and puts on a happy face for her family.

TANTALUST—Tantalus is a Greek mythological figure whom the gods punished by forcing him to stand in a pool of water. The fruit overhanging him exceeded his grasp, and water at his feet receded when he bent to quench his thirst. A person who has tantalust hungers to obtain emotional connection with a partner who is tantalizingly out of reach. The perpetrator may show sporadic warmth, but quickly withdraws it, and the lust for connection resumes.

Word variations: tantalusts, tantalusting

Holly's level of anxiety spikes when she and Todd have arguments, because he often walks out of the house and doesn't tell her where he's going or when he'll return. Sometimes he packs a bag and threatens to break up with her. Holly spends sleepless nights fretting about whether or not Todd will come back.

After a calm day during which they get along well, Holly asks Todd to pick up the clothing he has left all over their bedroom. He responds by accusing her of nagging him. When she tries to mollify him by offering to help him pick up, he screams at her to shut up and leave him alone.

Holly goes to the kitchen to begin preparing dinner, but soon she hears the front door open and close. She runs outside and pleads with Todd not to leave. "Todd, just come back and talk to me. We can work out our differences." Todd ignores her and screeches off in his car.

Holly runs up the stairs to their bedroom and opens Todd's chest of drawers. She's frantic to know if and when he'll return, and checks to find out if he has taken a clean shirt and change of underwear with him.

WHITE-FLAGGING—Abused partners wave the white flags of defeat when they accept their partners' abusive behavior. Sometimes white-flaggers apologize for "causing" their abusers' attacks. White-flagging downplays and excuses abuse and encourages more of it.

Word variations: white flag, white flags, white-flagged, white-flagger

Wanda and her husband, Sid, are on a friend's boat, cruising down the St. Johns River. In the cabin, the wine flows, the appetizers are laid out, and everyone is enjoying the ride.

Suddenly, the boat lurches and the appetizers spill to the floor. Wanda loses her balance and grips the table to keep from falling. She takes a few seconds to steady herself.

Sid grimaces at her. "Don't just stand there looking like a moron. Get down and pick up the food!" he commands and shoves her toward the floor.

Wanda bends down to collect the food, letting her hair cover her face to hide her humiliation. She tells Sid she's sorry, as if the accident is her fault, and she cleans up the mess. She spends the remainder of the boat ride in embarrassed silence as Sid basks in his feelings of superiority.

TAKING THE BLAME: CONFUSION AND INSECURITY

EDGY VIGIL—A state of intense dread and fear in anticipation of a partner's return home

Chuck gathered the courage to stand up to his wife, Valerie, the day before, after another one of her rages against him. Valerie is punishing him with stony silence for having the audacity to challenge her. She ignored him last night and left for work early in the morning before he woke up.

Later in the day, as Chuck waits for Valerie to return home, his chest is tight, his breathing is shallow, and sweat beads on his forehead. When he hears her car pull up in the driveway, his heart rate accelerates. He burrows down in his chair and tries to read, but anxiety tugs at him and his mind races with random thoughts.

I'll offer to cook dinner tonight or take her out to her favorite restaurant. Maybe she'll forgive me. He glances around the room and spies his muddy shoes by the front door. He sprints across the room and puts his shoes away. *I don't want to give her any more reasons to start in on me.* Chuck darts down the basement stairs to his home office. *She won't bother me if I'm working.*

Overcome with insecurity, Chuck is deeply ashamed for being so afraid of Valerie.

INTERNALIZING CRITICISM—When abused people believe their aggressors' criticism and absorb the critical voice into their own minds. Once internalized, the voice replaces affirming thoughts of self-worth with attacks on self-esteem, leading to anxiety, depression, self-loathing, and despair. Internalizing criticism works against the abused, even when their abusers are not present, or when the abused are no longer in abusive relationships.

Word variations: internalize criticism, internalizes criticism, internalized criticism

Natalie excelled in commercial art in school and opened her own graphic arts studio. Her talent and business acumen brought in contracts with local retail outfits and restaurants. Early in her relationship with Stephen, he seemed to support her accomplishments.

After they marry, Natalie wants to take out a loan to expand her studio and purchase the latest computer technology to keep up with her competition, but Stephen discourages her. "You'll just sink us into more debt with your lame-brained ideas," he warns her. "You got lucky when you opened your business. The contracts fell on your front door. You're kidding yourself if you think you'll ever be more than a graphic artist doing small jobs."

At first she disagrees with him, but over time he persists in tearing her down. She loses her confidence to take on new challenges and limits her work to small accounts. When business begins to fall off, she comes to believe Stephen is right that her business success was the result of luck, that she isn't capable.

Natalie closes her studio and works part-time out of her home. Stephen wins his way; he felt threatened by her success and wants her to be dependent on him, so she won't leave him.

MUDDLED—Bafflement over whether or not a mate's criticism is meant to be helpful or hurtful

Word variations: muddle, muddles, muddling

Tricia's head is swimming. She can't figure out if Corey's frequent disapproval of her lifestyle choices is meant to control her or is offered as constructive criticism. When they're together, Corey nitpicks her: "I want you to have a hard body, so you should go to the gym every day. Don't eat potato chips with your sandwich; they're not healthy. You need to improve your makeup. Stop smacking your food. You shouldn't be wearing flip-flops. You're letting yourself go; is that what happens in relationships?"

Sometimes Corey compliments Tricia. He tells her that she's smart, beautiful, and has a lot of heart. His push-pull treatment confuses her. She acknowledges that she has room for improvement, but his faultfinding makes her feel dejected, unattractive, and unmotivated. "You say you're trying to help me, but if you don't like so many things about me, why are you with me?" Tricia asks Corey.

He responds, "I just want you to make better choices for your own good."

Corey's statement does nothing to clarify Tricia's bewilderment. Do his judgments mean that if she doesn't live up to his expectations, he won't love her anymore? Or, if she manages to fulfill all his requirements, will he accept her and love the new and improved version of her? To keep his love, will she have to continue to submit to his rulings? When does it all end?

Tricia doesn't realize that Corey's reproach won't end until he sees and accepts that it is a result of his discontent with himself. He feels she is a reflection of him, and his feelings of personal inadequacy drive his need to be perfect. Rather than face his own shortcomings, he criticizes her.

Muddled

MUZZLED—A self-imposed gag order to refrain from voicing personal opinions, thoughts, ideas, or experiences. Why? To avoid a mate's criticism or demeaning treatment, especially when other people are around.

Word variations: muzzle, muzzles, muzzling

Leslie is shy and uncomfortable when she is the center of attention, but her self-confidence increases when she expresses herself and people support and validate her. Her partner, Charlie, uses her timidity to gain a sense of power and control over her. He gets perverse enjoyment when she speaks out and he discredits and silences her.

One evening, Leslie and Charlie attend a party at a friend's home. Leslie wants to engage in conversation with a group of friends, so she steels her courage to describe her experience with learning how to snow ski. "The first time I went skiing, I didn't latch my left ski properly, and the ski fell off in the middle of a downhill run," she recounts. "I found myself spontaneously learning how to snowboard."

People laugh, which encourages Leslie to continue, but Charlie cuts her off. "Okay, Leslie. That's enough about your boring ski trip. No one wants to listen to your idiotic maneuvers."

Leslie is mortified. Charlie has turned her fun to embarrassment. She waits until Charlie walks to the bar for another drink to resume talking. Just before he returns, she stops talking and asks someone in the group a question to take the focus off of herself.

If only Leslie knew that Charlie uses her to feed his obsessive need to feel smarter than other people.

Muzzled

OUTCAST—When partners are so traumatized by their abusive mates that they see themselves as exiles in their own communities. The outcasts' deep shame makes them feel awkward and self-conscious in public. They imagine that everyone looks down on them because they are so worthless. It's not probable that everyone passes judgment on those who feel like outcasts, but an exception might be the few people who go along with the abuser's hateful gossip about the abused.

Lionel instructs his wife, Gisele, to stay home while he takes their two children to their son's basketball game, because he doesn't want to be seen with her. Barring her from her son's game is typical of his ruthless treatment, which has grown worse during their eighteen-year marriage.

Gisele doesn't realize that Lionel is sadistic and derives pleasure from inflicting emotional pain on her. She has adopted as her own what she believes is his rightfully low opinion of her, and she blames herself for his maltreatment. She is torn between her insecurity and her desire to see her son play basketball. She goes to the game.

When Gisele walks into the gymnasium where the game is in progress, she imagines that everyone is staring at her disapprovingly. She thinks they know how unhappy Lionel is with her, because she is pathetic. Gisele sits by herself in a dark corner of the bleachers. When another parent comes by to say hello and asks if she can sit beside her, Gisele weeps in gratitude at such a kind gesture.

SHELL-SHOCKED—Intense and contradictory emotions that lead to irrational and obsessive thoughts and mind-numbing confusion. Shell-shocked people live with a high level of fear and anxiety, as if they are in a war zone. Sometimes they stare into space, unable to make sense of their feelings.

Hediyeh's husband, Farhoud, jerks the bedroom curtains open early on a Saturday morning. He orders her to get out of bed, even though a stomach virus has kept her up much of the night. She is exhausted in mind and body after years of enduring Farhoud's searing contempt, tirades, and directives.

"The children are downstairs and they need their breakfast," he states with a total lack of consideration for her illness. "Get some things done around the house today." Farhoud tells her he will not be home until nightfall.

Hediyeh has long decided that being submissive to him is the best way to keep the peace in their family. She pushes herself up and props her body against the headboard. After breathing deeply and letting out a shuddering sigh, she wills herself to fight the day's battle. Her eyes transfixed on the wall in front of her, she stumbles through the chaos in her mind: *Am I being unreasonable to want to stay in bed? Is Farhoud out of line for leaving me when I'm ill? There's got to be a reason why he treats me so poorly. Maybe he put poison in my food to get rid of me. Surely he wouldn't go that far—or would he? It's my fault. If I am going to be married to this man, I can't get sick.*

WALKING ON THIN ICE—To proceed very cautiously with words and actions when an abusive mate is close by. One wrong move may result in plunging into emotional ice water.

When Buddy is around Alma, he is meticulously careful about what he says and does, so he won't provoke her volatile temper and scathing criticism. He compliments her, helps her with the cooking and housework, and takes her out for gourmet dinners. Buddy constantly assesses Alma's moods. When he senses tension building between them, he goes along with her, regardless of who is right or wrong or how it affects him.

For months, Buddy has been looking forward to a deep-sea fishing trip off the Florida Keys with three of his boyhood friends. He has been extra attentive to Alma in the weeks before the trip, so he can enjoy the five-day excursion without worrying about her retaliation when he returns.

Several days before he is scheduled to leave, Alma's mood takes a downturn and she complains about everything he does, which increases Buddy's anxiety about his vacation.

The day before his trip, Buddy returns to the house after working out at the gym and sees a pile of clothes by the trash bin. When he gets up closer, he realizes the clothes belong to him. He takes a deep breath, closes his eyes, and exhales. "What have I done now?" he says out loud to himself.

He trudges into the house and asks Alma what happened. "I'm sick and tired of your messy closet, so I threw away your clothes," she huffs and walks off.

Buddy knows that if he stands up to Alma and returns the clothes to his closet, they will have an argument that will leave her angry with him and sabotage his fishing trip. He gets some trash bags from the house and puts his clothes in the bags. He stores them in the garage instead of returning them to his closet.

Walking On Thin Ice

Giving Yourself Away: Compromising Personal Values

COUNTERABUSE—When abused partners have tried and failed to improve their mates' behavior, they go against their personal values and resort to their mates' abusive tactics. Counterabuse not only condones abusive behavior, but it also encourages the abuser to shift blame onto the counterabuser.

Word variations: counterabuses, counterabused, counterabuser

Sydney is frazzled from putting up with Trey's rage and persecution of her. In an attempt to cope with him and improve their relationship, she has given in, apologized, argued, threatened, doled out punishment, withheld affection, and tried to talk with him in a reasonable manner, but nothing works.

Sydney resorts to the same abusive tactics Trey uses on her. One afternoon during a quarrel, she screams vulgar insults and accusations at him. She turns over a chair and shoves books and magazines off of the coffee table and onto the floor. She grabs a lamp and throws it at him, but the lamp misses and crashes against the wall.

Afterward, Sydney has serious misgivings about her behavior and is down on herself. Every time she complains about Trey's mistreatment, he brings up her tirade as proof of her immaturity and poor judgment.

GOLDEN CHAINS—To get caught up in the status, wealth, power, and luxury that come with a relationship, but at the expense of emotional health and well-being

Word variations: live in golden chains, lives in golden chains, living in golden chains, lived in golden chains

Joanie is married to Rhoda, the manager of a billion-dollar hedge fund. They have a seaside vacation home in Palm Beach, Florida, attend elegant parties with high-status people, and make trips abroad.

When Joanie and Rhoda first met, Joanie catered to wealthy clientele as a high-end, designer style consultant at Saks Fifth Avenue. Joanie envied the lavish lives of her clients, but believed she wasn't capable of achieving such an existence on her own. Joanie was thrilled when she found a life partner who also lived the lifestyle Joanie desired.

After their marriage, Rhoda encourages Joanie to quit her job and assures Joanie that she will support her financially. Before long, however, Joanie realizes that Rhoda is not the exciting, interesting, and loving woman Joanie thought she married. Rhoda is arrogant, insensitive, and self-focused. She treats Joanie as if she is an accessory that exists for the sole purpose of catering to Rhoda's every need.

Joanie won't leave Rhoda, however. She trades off serenity, personal fulfillment, and self-respect for a sense of financial security, prestige, and a luxurious lifestyle. Joanie develops migraine headaches and has chronic anxiety. Her frequent shopping excursions to buy the latest designer clothing and jewelry help assuage her anxiety, but not for long. She endures the emptiness inside her heart by drinking an excessive amount of wine every night and fantasizing about the day she will say good-bye to Rhoda. *She'll be sorry about the way she treated me when I'm gone*, Joanie muses.

MIMICKING—Going against personal values and beliefs to imitate a partner's destructive behaviors, in an effort to cope with an abusive relationship or gain the abuser's attention and approval. Behaviors include alcohol and drug abuse, illegal activities, and other objectionable actions toward oneself or others.

Word variations: mimic, mimics, mimicked

Carolyn loves Andy, but she strains to cope with his overbearing nature and self-defeating conduct, which make her feel distant from him.

One night at a party, Andy disappears. When she sees him going into a bathroom with other people, she knocks on the door and asks to be let in. Inside, there is a hand mirror on the counter with white powder laid out in lines. "Go ahead, give it a try. I think you'll like it," Andy encourages her.

Carolyn replies, "I don't know. Doesn't it make your nose bleed?"

Andy counters, "It's not cut with anything that would irritate your nose. It's no big deal."

Carolyn has never used drugs before, but she wants to show Andy how fun-loving she can be. She reasons that if they share experiences, they will grow closer as a couple.

Carolyn snorts lines of cocaine, and the drug keeps her up all night. In the morning, her body aches, her nose burns, and she is weary from lack of sleep. She regrets using cocaine and realizes that her involvement in Andy's self-destructive behavior does not strengthen their emotional connection.

SACRIFICIAL LAMB—Is it necessary to accept a mate's abuse and give up emotional health and well-being to keep the family together? Sacrificial lambs say yes for several reasons. They may believe that an intact family is best for the children, or that marriage vows must be honored. They may consider divorce against their religious or spiritual beliefs. They may fear that they can't make it on their own. Whatever the reason, the choice is theirs.

Katie is married to Gabe, a city council member who is a pillar of the community. Together they have three school-age children. He is active in his church and the leader of an organization that mentors young people.

When Gabe is away from the public eye, however, he treats the family pet better than he does his wife. He bullies Katie with his merciless demands, explodes into rants against her at a moment's notice, and calls her derogatory names, especially in front of their children.

Katie is ashamed to reveal to her family and friends the truth about how Gabe treats her, because others see only his polished image. They would be shocked if they knew the truth. Regardless of the circumstances, she believes that an unbroken family is essential to the children's proper growth and development.

Ironically, Katie is working against her objective by staying with a psychologically impaired man who refuses to get professional help. Her goal is to act in the best interests of her family, but every day she sacrifices her and her children's emotional, mental, and physical health.

SELF-DESTRUCTIVE COPING—When abused partners attempt to numb their emotional pain with injurious, obsessive, or addictive behaviors. Self-destructive coping may include substance abuse; excessive gambling, pornography or video games; overspending and credit card debt; self-injury; or any other behavior used to avoid the truth, postpone anxiety, or punish oneself. Although self-destructive coping may provide a temporary escape from emotional pain, the magnitude of the pain increases.

Morris's level of anxiety goes way up when his partner, Kevin, stays out all night. Kevin tells Morris he goes to a local bar with his buddies, but he slips into their house at five o'clock in the morning. Morris knows the bars close at two, so where is Kevin for three hours?

Morris gives up questioning Kevin; his evasiveness and defensive stance frustrate Morris. Instead of seeking the help of a psychotherapist and standing up to Kevin about his disloyal and abusive behavior, Morris turns to alcohol. A couple of drinks every evening increases to half a bottle of whiskey, when Kevin goes out at night. Morris's inebriation only provides a momentary respite from his emotional pain, however. In the morning, his anxiety comes rushing back.

TRIGGERING—The tension buildup before an abusive attack can be like the pressure of a head vise. The person who anticipates being on the receiving end of the attack may intentionally or unintentionally provoke the abuser to get relief. Sometimes the abused person spurs on a physical attack to gain hard evidence of abuse.

Word variations: trigger, triggers, triggered

Carmen can't endure the unpredictability of Patrick's fiery temper. She knows he will erupt at any moment, and she wants to be done with it. Her excruciating anxiety causes her to lose her composure. She shouts at him, "What have I done now? Did I look at you the wrong way? I'm sick and tired of your moods. You make my life miserable. All you think about is yourself!"

Patrick grabs Carmen by the arms and shrieks obscenities at her. They have a violent argument. Carmen weeps uncontrollably and runs out of the house. She walks around the neighborhood in a distressed state for an hour.

When Carmen returns, Patrick has locked her out of the house even though it has started to rain. He won't let her in until she apologizes to him. When the episode ends and Carmen is back in the house, she is somewhat relieved that he may be calm for a while, but she is also deeply ashamed that she compromises herself to cope with Patrick's maltreatment.

UNPLUGGED—The inability to be emotionally present for friends and family members because of the inner chaos and anguish of an abusive relationship. People who are unplugged seldom have fulfilling relationships with other people because having an abusive partner requires all their emotional and physical energy. Unplugged parents can't always nourish the emotional needs of their children.

Word variations: unplug, unplugs, unplugging

Aliyah talks on the phone with her younger sister, Destiny, who knows about Aliyah's abusive husband, Dion. "That's not all he did. Let me tell you the latest," Aliyah rambles on. "He came home in a foul mood, and wouldn't speak to me. When I asked him what was wrong with him, he said 'This is what's wrong.' Before I could stop him, he took the used cooking oil from the chicken I baked for dinner and dumped it all over my Louis Vuitton handbag. Can you imagine that anyone could do such a thing?"

Before Destiny can react, Aliyah continues her frenetic rundown of Dion's offenses. Destiny manages to say one or two words before Aliyah breaks in again. Destiny waits for her sister to calm down so Destiny can share her news that she got a coveted job promotion and large salary increase, but Aliyah is in no mind to think about anyone but herself.

Destiny decides to hold off on her announcement. She is reluctant to bring up her success when Aliyah is overwrought.

A SECRET LIFE: CONCEALING THE TROUBLE

FANTASIZING—When an abused person has recurrent and elaborate daydreams about implausible changes in either the abusive partner or the relationship, such as revenge or a happy ending. Fantasizers only dream; they take no constructive action to address the abuse, protect themselves, or get help.

Word variations: fantasy, fantasies, fantasized, fantasizer

Marge stays with her abusive husband, Bradley, because she has a low opinion of herself, lacks self-confidence, and fears life on her own. To cope with her angst and despair, she fantasizes about an imaginary lover who will rescue her from Bradley.

In Marge's fantasy, Bradley watches in desperation as she rides away in an expensive car driven by a rich and handsome man who adores her. The dream version of Bradley is insane with jealousy and remorseful about the way he treated her.

In another fantasy, Marge suffers a heart attack in response to Bradley's abuse. As the ambulance takes her to the hospital with Bradley by her side, he realizes how awful he has been to her and how much he loves her. He begs for her forgiveness, she recuperates, and once again they are blissfully in love.

FICTIONAL THINKING—To create fiction about oneself, a partner, or a relationship and see the fiction as truth. Fictional thinkers bury the facts with their stories and believe what they *want* to believe. When friends or family members see the truth and try to expose it, fictional thinkers stick with their stories or craft more stories to refute the evidence. In many cases, fictional thinking is what draws a person into an abusive relationship. Fictional thinkers become truthful thinkers when they muster the courage to accept painful realities.

Word variations: fictional thinker, fictional thoughts

Alicia and Chase have been together for three years, even though he cheats on her, lies to her, and complains about her weight, choices, and opinions. At times, he buys her expensive gifts, helps her pay her credit card debt, and takes her on extravagant vacations to foreign countries.

Alicia believes that Chase is her soul mate and that one day they will marry and he will transform into a dependable, kind, and loving partner. Alicia's girlfriends warn her about Chase, but she tells them that they don't know him like she does and haven't seen his better qualities.

Alicia doesn't tell her girlfriends that she secretly blames herself for the relationship's problems and considers herself lucky that a wealthy, debonair, and attractive man like Chase is with her. She endures the emotional pain he inflicts on her and waits for the day he will change.

MASKING—The unwillingness to acknowledge the presence of emotional abuse in a relationship. The abused minimize or deny their mates' abusive behavior and act as if their relationships are normal or will eventually improve. They conceal their torment and deny the reality of deeply troubled unions with their partners. They may see themselves as morally superior to their abusive mates.

Word variations: mask, masks, masked

Candace won't see Jürgen's belligerence, groundless accusations, unreasonable demands, and suffocating know-it-all attitude as emotional abuse. She accepts that he is a difficult person, but she plasters over his abuse with a variety of excuses and explanations.

Sometimes Candace attributes Jürgen's behavior to the highs and lows of marriage. At other times, she relies on a male stereotype that describes men as unable to talk about their tender emotions, so they express them in "manly" ways. Candace believes she has more maturity and emotional strength than Jürgen does, so she "takes the high road" and tolerates him as if he were a well-meaning but willful teenager.

Meanwhile, Candace stays in a heightened state of anxiety and has episodes of debilitating fatigue that have no physical cause.

SELF-ISOLATION—The avoidance of friends and family members who know about an abusive mate. They ask too many questions, such as "How can you stand the way you are treated?" and "Do you realize how concerned we are about you?" Self-isolators can't hide their toxic relationships when they spend time with people who know them well.

Word variations: self-isolator, self-isolating

Victoria loves Danny and hopes they can work out their differences. She believes that he is sullen, controlling, and short-tempered because he grew up with an alcoholic father who didn't take much interest in him. When Danny doesn't get his way, he shouts accusations at Victoria, calls her hurtful names, and destroys items in their home. He won't let her go anywhere without him, even to the grocery store.

When Victoria confronts him about his behavior, he breaks down into a teary apology and tells her sad stories about his childhood. "You're the only one who really understands me," he whines. "I can't trust anyone but you." Danny threatens to kill himself if she leaves him.

Victoria has a large family that has witnessed Danny's temper tantrums at gatherings. They ask questions and express their concern when Victoria visits, which is less and less often. She makes excuses so she won't have to attend family events.

Victoria puts up with Danny's abuse because she believes he loves her, and she doesn't want to hurt him like others have. She lives in the illusion that if she loves him enough, he will become a sensible, even-tempered, and caring partner.

STAGING—To cover up emotional battering at home, the abused person colludes with the perpetrator to present a united front of "happy couple" when the two of them are with others.

Word variations: stage, stages, staged, stager

Nina depletes herself to meet Paul's oppressive mandates and suffers from his wrath if she doesn't. On their way to meet Nina's parents for Sunday lunch, Nina weeps while Paul scowls. Her nerves are shot after yet another one of Paul's jealous fits, in which he charges her with being interested in a man she talked with at church.

When they get to the restaurant, Nina asks Paul to go inside and meet her parents while she stays in the car to freshen her makeup. "Tell them I'm on the phone," Nina suggests.

As Nina works to conceal her puffy nose and red eyes, Paul transforms into the picture of joviality and greets Nina's parents with bright-eyed enthusiasm. "Nina got a call from her boss on the way over, and she's finishing up her conversation with him," Paul lies. "She'll be in shortly."

When Nina walks in and smiles at her parents, her mother's face falls. "My allergies are acting up again," Nina fibs. "I probably look worse than I feel."

THE CENTER WILL NOT HOLD: FALLING IN DEEPER

CATCHING THE FLU (INFLUENCE)—The emotional condition of people who are so influenced by their abusive mates that they surrender themselves and leave a void for their mates to think *for* them. Those who catch the flu internalize criticism and disregard their needs, feelings, values, intuition, and cherished beliefs. They lose the confidence to make it on their own and become dependent on their abusers. At times they think they may be losing touch with reality, but they are too scared and ashamed to reveal their burdens. They become as emotionally desolate as their abusive mates.

Word variations: catch the flu, caught the flu

Jeanine radiates vitality as a popular student and cheerleader for her high school football team. Her wholesome beauty brings the attention of Johnny, senior class president and debate team captain. They both get scholarships to reputable universities and marry after college.

When their children are born, however, Johnny loses interest in their relationship because Jeanine can no longer give him all of her time and attention. Her focus on caring for the children uncovers a painful emotional injury from Johnny's childhood that will eventually destroy their marriage. When he was a child, his mother shamed him and called him a sissy for needing her love and attention. He learned that he would get hurt if he revealed his tender feelings. When Jeanine's attention turns to the children, Johnny feels the same rejection from Jeanine as he did from his mother.

Johnny's feelings of rejection turn into disdain for his wife. Jeanine is the target for all the hurt, anger, and resentment he felt for his mother when he was a child. He blames Jeanine for his discontent, blasts her with criticism, belittles her decisions, and is chronically unreliable.

Now in their early fifties, their love is long gone. Jeanine stays with Johnny, however, because she has never known any other life and is concerned that she is too old to start over with another man. Jeanine works hard to please him so he won't abandon her for another woman. After being with Johnny for years, her sense of self-worth is abysmal. She lacks the confidence to make even the smallest decision without him. No longer interested in activities that once gave her pleasure, she puts on weight and wears shapeless, unattractive clothes. She doesn't understand what happened to her marriage and blames herself for Johnny's contempt. At times, Jeanine feels as though she is losing her emotional stability, and has trouble getting out of bed in the morning.

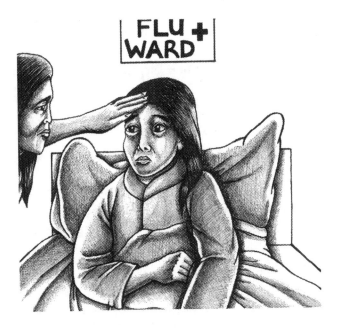

DETERIORATION OF EMOTIONAL, MENTAL, AND PHYSICAL WELL-BEING

—The effect of an abusive relationship on the abused person's general health. Emotional decline includes anxiety, shame, self-reproach, despair, apathy, and the erosion of self. Mental decline includes depression, symptoms of post-traumatic stress disorder, stress-induced psychosis, and suicide ideation. Physical decline includes headaches, body aches, gastrointestinal distress, fatigue, and other bodily ailments that are mentally induced.

Ginger has been married to Bubba, an emotionally abusive man, for twenty-eight years. She is a shell of her former self. Her natural cheerfulness and optimism have turned to indifference and hopelessness. She used to love working at a women's boutique, volunteering at a children's charity, and designing beautiful needlepoint pillows, but now she stays home all day and watches television.

Ginger suffers from panic attacks and has chronic aches and pains. She has long wanted to divorce Bubba, but she fears she can't make it on her own. She fantasizes about the day Bubba will die and she can afford to live alone on their retirement savings. Meanwhile Ginger stays with Bubba, who she can't stand, and her health continues to deteriorate.

GOING DOWN WITH THE SHIP—To stay in an abusive relationship because of a belief that parting means personal failure due to weakness, lack of courage, or desertion of commitments and responsibility. Those who go down with the ship sometimes make futile efforts to save their unions as the relationships sink deeper into despair.

Word variations: go down with the ship, goes down with the ship, went down with the ship

Amelia endures enormous stress in her marriage to Quincy, a narcissistic man who cares only about himself, but she believes that ending their marriage is equivalent to giving up. Failure is not an option for her. She worked twelve hours a day, six days a week to become a partner in a prestigious law firm, and she applied the same approach to her pursuit of Quincy, who is chief executive officer of a major corporation.

Amelia is proud of her tough-mindedness and believes she can handle backbreaking pressure in her work and in her marriage. "I've labored for years to get where I am, and I'm not throwing in the towel," she tells her friends. Public recognition for her success gives her personal satisfaction, but her achievements go only as far as her social status and material wealth. Every day, Amelia pays an increasingly higher price with her emotional health and well-being.

HOOKED ON HOPE—To cling to the expectation that a partner will change for the better, when there is no real and lasting evidence that change will happen. Unhappy partners pin their hopes on the possibility that their mates will become aware of harmful behavior, feel shame and remorse, and transform their ways. Hope hookers give their mates the power to resolve issues and wait for that resolution. They don't realize that people who mistreat others don't change easily. They will wait forever if they keep issuing more chances that lead to the same disappointing results.

Word variations: hooks on hope, hooking on hope, hope hooker

Derrick is a makeup artist who lives in Los Angeles when he meets Simon, an actor, at a film shoot in New York. The two men fall in love and commute between New York and California for a year, until Derrick moves into Simon's home in Greenwich Village. Simon presses Derrick to get married. Derrick agrees, even though Derrick wants a longer relationship before they commit to each other.

At the wedding, Simon humiliates Derrick by shoving cake in his face during the cake-cutting ceremony, but Derrick chalks up the incident to Simon's wedding nerves. Life is blissful during the first few months of their marriage. Simon's career as an actor in a popular television series opens up doors to celebrity friends and trendy nightlife. Derrick enjoys doing things for Simon, and Simon comes to depend on him.

But Simon's requests turn into demands. At three o'clock one morning, Simon arrives home with friends who are drunk and hungry, wakes up Derrick, and orders him to cook steaks. Simon is irritated, but he gets up and cooks the meal.

A couple of weeks later, Simon mortifies Derrick at a private party by pushing him into the pool with his clothes on. Simon laughs. "You look like a wet rat!"

Derrick is shaken and confronts Simon about his disrespectful treatment when they return home. Derrick tells Simon he loves him and relishes their life together, but he will leave if Simon doesn't improve his conduct toward Derrick. Simon apologizes and asks for another chance.

Four years go by, during which Simon continues to sabotage their relationship by mistreating Derrick. Derrick continues to give Simon passes on his behavior and waits for the day when Simon will change. Derrick believes he has been good to Simon for a long time, and Simon owes him a lot. "Sooner or later, Simon will realize how much I do for him, and he will treat me well," Derrick reasons.

Meanwhile, Derrick is deeply conflicted and unhappy with their relationship and with himself.

HOUSE OF MIRRORS—A house in which two contradictory worlds exist. From the outside looking in, the image is picture-perfect. On the inside, however, the picture is distorted like a funhouse mirror into a living hell of emotional abuse. Existence in the two dichotomous worlds may cause the abused person to doubt his or her own sanity.

Sameera and Sanjay are both highly accomplished physicians who work for a prestigious world health organization. They are lauded in the community for their research work. Everyone sees them as a contented, attractive and successful couple.

Behind closed doors, however, Sanjay keeps Sameera in constant turmoil. He is uptight, cold, and egotistical. When she rebuffs his tyranny, he admonishes her and simmers in silence for days. When she misunderstands him and asks him to clarify, he snaps at her and insists she doesn't listen to him. At times, he deliberately distorts her reality with lies and denial. Often she cannot even determine the basis of their arguments.

The more Sameera labors to gain Sanjay's approval, the more he eludes her. Their interaction often boggles her mind, and she teeters on the brink of emotional stability.

PSYCHOSOMATIC ILLNESS—Mental stress that manifests in physical illness, such as frequent colds, stomach ailments, headaches, or body pains

Sandy's husband, Abe, drinks his first vodka when he gets home from work at 5:30 p.m. every day. As the evening wears on and he drinks more vodka, his behavior switches from curt indifference to hostile aggression. Abe uses Sandy as an emotional punching bag to vent his anger and frustration, and he refuses to acknowledge his addiction to alcohol and get into recovery. Their twelve-year-old son and fifteen-year-old daughter know to stay out of sight by the time their father has finished his second vodka.

Sandy, however, can't escape from Abe so easily. He often picks a fight with her before bedtime, and she associates the bedroom with nighttime arguments that agitate her and prevent her from sleeping. She has troubling memories of his insistence on sex after he treats her with callous disregard. Most nights she stays in a tense, fetal position and fears that any movement will wake him.

Sandy has a stiff neck, debilitating joint pain, and recurring upper respiratory infections, but her doctors can't find a medical cause for her ailments.

PART III

ASSESSMENT, PROTECTION, AND TREATMENT

CHAPTER FIVE

Gauge Your Relationship and Its Effects on You

Emotional abuse is often hard to spot in a relationship. Most abusers don't take responsibility for mistreating others, and they commonly pin the blame on abuse recipients. The abused one may be overcome with self-doubt and confused about what is causing the trouble.

Asking yourself specific questions and contemplating the answers will help you gain clarity about your relationship. If you answer yes to any of the questions in the following three quizzes, there may be emotional abuse in your relationship. I encourage you to talk with a qualified psychotherapist who is experienced in treating emotional abuse survivors. The psychotherapist can advise you about therapy resources for your abusive partner as well.

Quiz #1: Is Your Mate Emotionally Abusive?

Are you distressed because your partner resists your efforts to resolve disagreements or relationship issues?	☐ Yes ☐ No
Does your partner believe that you should do what he or she tells you to do?	☐ Yes ☐ No
Does your partner disrespect you?	☐ Yes ☐ No
Does your partner criticize, mock, or discount you when you express your opinions, needs, and feelings?	☐ Yes ☐ No
Does your partner fail to follow through on his or her promises to you?	☐ Yes ☐ No
Do you often feel empty or confused when you and your partner discuss an issue between you?	☐ Yes ☐ No
Does your partner often blame you when you are not at fault?	☐ Yes ☐ No
Does your partner make excuses for behavior that is hurtful to you?	☐ Yes ☐ No
Does your partner make you the butt of his or her jokes?	☐ Yes ☐ No
Does your partner hurt you and then act as if he or she did nothing to upset you?	☐ Yes ☐ No
Does your partner put his or her needs before yours?	☐ Yes ☐ No

Do you have to push your partner to spend time with you?	☐ Yes ☐ No
Does your partner go away for long periods of time without telling you where he or she is going or where he or she has been?	☐ Yes ☐ No
Is it difficult to talk freely to your partner without screening or holding back on what you want to say?	☐ Yes ☐ No
Does your partner often criticize what you do and how you do it?	☐ Yes ☐ No
Does your partner discourage you from spending time with your friends and family members?	☐ Yes ☐ No
Are there discrepancies between what your partner says and what he or she does?	☐ Yes ☐ No
Does your partner tell you that you are overly sensitive?	☐ Yes ☐ No
Does your partner make you account for every penny you spend, prevent your access to financial resources, or deny you the opportunity to work outside the home?	☐ Yes ☐ No
Does your partner criticize or tease you about your illness or disability, or prevent you from taking care of your special needs?	☐ Yes ☐ No
Does your partner criticize or tease you about your religious or spiritual beliefs, or try to stop you from practicing your faith?	☐ Yes ☐ No

Does your partner criticize or tease you about your race, culture, or sexual orientation?	☐ Yes ☐ No
Does your partner often remember an incident or experience quite differently than you do and refuse to consider your version of the experience?	☐ Yes ☐ No
Does your partner lie to you?	☐ Yes ☐ No
Does your partner's behavior embarrass or humiliate you?	☐ Yes ☐ No
Is your partner having an emotional or sexual affair?	☐ Yes ☐ No
Does your partner insist you have sex on demand or have sex in ways that hurt, humiliate, or scare you?	☐ Yes ☐ No
Have you ever been afraid to say no to sex with your partner?	☐ Yes ☐ No
Does your partner treat you like an inferior person or a child?	☐ Yes ☐ No
Does your partner insist that you spend all your spare time with him or her?	☐ Yes ☐ No
Does your partner downplay your accomplishments?	☐ Yes ☐ No
Does your partner discourage you from pursuing your personal interests and aspirations?	☐ Yes ☐ No

Does your partner use religion to control and manipulate you into doing what he or she believes you should do?	☐ Yes ☐ No
Does your partner give you the silent treatment or withhold approval, affection, sex, or money to get his or her way?	☐ Yes ☐ No
Does your partner threaten you when he or she doesn't get his or her way?	☐ Yes ☐ No
Does your partner call you hurtful names and try to convince you that the names are merely harmless jokes that you should not take seriously?	☐ Yes ☐ No
Is your partner's anger toward you or someone else an extreme overreaction to the cause, which is often insignificant?	☐ Yes ☐ No
Is your partner violent with you, your children, other people, pets, items, or property?	☐ Yes ☐ No
Are you concerned that your partner is hurting your children or will hurt your children?	☐ Yes ☐ No
Does your partner's behavior scare you or your children?	☐ Yes ☐ No
Does your partner tell lies about you to your children?	☐ Yes ☐ No
Since you have been in your current relationship, have there been any changes in your children's behaviors that concern you?	☐ Yes ☐ No

Quiz #2: How Has Your Relationship Affected You?

Do you have a higher level of anxiety right before your partner gets home?	☐ Yes ☐ No
Do you doubt yourself a lot when you interact with your partner?	☐ Yes ☐ No
Do you feel a need to screen what you say and how you speak to your partner for fear that he or she will criticize you or get angry?	☐ Yes ☐ No
Do you often feel confused and upset after talking with your partner?	☐ Yes ☐ No
Do you have difficulty relaxing and sleeping at night after interacting with your partner?	☐ Yes ☐ No
Is it difficult to make simple decisions independent of your partner?	☐ Yes ☐ No
Do you often feel sad or depressed as a result of your relationship?	☐ Yes ☐ No
Do you feel like you're stuck in a relationship that's not good for you?	☐ Yes ☐ No
Have you lost interest in what you used to love doing?	☐ Yes ☐ No
Do you spend an excessive amount of time trying to figure out what you could have done to anger your partner?	☐ Yes ☐ No

Do you keep quiet in public when you have something to say, for fear of being criticized or humiliated by your partner?	☐ Yes ☐ No
Do you hear your partner's criticism of you in your own head?	☐ Yes ☐ No
Does your partner provoke you, leading you to behave in ways that you later feel ashamed of?	☐ Yes ☐ No
Has the quality of your relationships with friends and family members decreased since you've been in your current relationship?	☐ Yes ☐ No
Are you staying with an abusive partner because you believe that no one else would want you?	☐ Yes ☐ No
Are you staying with an abusive partner because he or she has convinced you that you cannot afford to live without his or her financial support?	☐ Yes ☐ No
If you have an illness, disability, or special needs, do you struggle with taking care of your needs because your partner criticizes you or won't help you?	☐ Yes ☐ No
Do you suspect the cause of your more frequent colds, aches and pains, and other ailments may be due to the stress in your relationship?	☐ Yes ☐ No
Is your current relationship hurting your children?	☐ Yes ☐ No

Are you often confused about whether your partner is trying to help or hurt you?	☐ Yes ☐ No
Are you often confused about whether or not you should take the blame for issues in your relationship?	☐ Yes ☐ No
Do you sit and stare for long periods of time, unable to make sense of what's happening in your relationship?	☐ Yes ☐ No
Do you spend long periods of time thinking about what happened between you and your partner?	☐ Yes ☐ No
Do you spend a great deal of time mentally going over what you wish you could say to your partner, even though you never actually say it?	☐ Yes ☐ No
Do you have obsessive thoughts about seeking revenge against your partner?	☐ Yes ☐ No
Do you have obsessive thoughts about hurting yourself or your partner?	☐ Yes ☐ No
Are you afraid of doing anything that might upset your partner?	☐ Yes ☐ No
Do you often feel angry, fearful, or agitated when you are around your partner?	☐ Yes ☐ No
Does the stress caused by your relationship make you feel as if you're going to lose your mind?	☐ Yes ☐ No

QUIZ #3: ARE YOU CONTRIBUTING TO YOUR MATE'S ABUSIVE TREATMENT?

Do you tolerate, downplay, or ignore your mate's abusive treatment or behavior?	☐ Yes ☐ No
Do you make excuses for your partner's bad behavior?	☐ Yes ☐ No
Are you quick to defend your partner or your relationship when family members and friends express their concern about the way your partner treats you?	☐ Yes ☐ No
Are you confused about whether or not you are the cause of the problems in your relationship?	☐ Yes ☐ No
Do you take the blame for issues in your relationship even though you feel you are not to blame?	☐ Yes ☐ No
Do you constantly think about how to please your partner?	☐ Yes ☐ No
Do you go to extremes to gain your partner's approval, even though your partner doesn't seem to appreciate your efforts?	☐ Yes ☐ No
Do you stay awake at night wondering where your partner is, or waiting for him or her to get home?	☐ Yes ☐ No
Do you refrain from speaking when your partner's behavior upsets you?	☐ Yes ☐ No

Do you give in to your partner to prevent a fight?	☐ Yes ☐ No
Do you have sex with your partner to prevent a fight?	☐ Yes ☐ No
Do you allow your partner to coerce you into sex acts that hurt or humiliate you?	☐ Yes ☐ No
Do you believe if you make fundamental changes in your character traits or looks, your partner will love you, or you will be worthy of your partner's love?	☐ Yes ☐ No
Do you try to please your partner by going against your own values and beliefs or behaving in ways that are destructive to yourself or other people?	☐ Yes ☐ No
Do you use drugs, alcohol, gambling, excessive spending, or any other obsessive activity to escape from painful feelings about your relationship?	☐ Yes ☐ No
Have you given up your hopes, dreams, or aspirations against your will since you have been in your current relationship?	☐ Yes ☐ No
Do you retaliate against your partner by using some of the same abusive tactics he or she uses on you?	☐ Yes ☐ No
Do you wish your partner would physically harm you so you would have evidence of his or her abusive treatment of you?	☐ Yes ☐ No

Do you tolerate your partner's cheating on you and refusing to get professional help?	☐ Yes ☐ No
Do you tolerate your partner's lies?	☐ Yes ☐ No
Do you tolerate your partner's lack of availability for you and your children?	☐ Yes ☐ No
If your partner abuses your children, do you tolerate the abuse?	☐ Yes ☐ No
Do you act as if everything is okay in your relationship when you're hurting inside?	☐ Yes ☐ No
Do you isolate yourself from friends or family members who know you have a difficult relationship?	☐ Yes ☐ No
Have you decided to stay in an abusive relationship because you fear you can't make it on your own?	☐ Yes ☐ No
Have you accepted your abusive relationship as your fate and given up on trying to improve your life situation?	☐ Yes ☐ No
Do you find yourself going from one difficult relationship to another?	☐ Yes ☐ No

CHAPTER SIX

Protection

FINDING YOUR VOICE

The key answer to why people abuse others is: *because they can.*
So be assertive and act quickly to set limits. You will send the
message that you are not an easy target and will no longer accept
the abuse. Asserting yourself will help to release pent-up emotions
and boost your confidence and self-respect.

Effective communication means respect for yourself and the
other person. Use "I" statements to describe how the abusive
behavior affects you. An example of an "I" statement is: "I feel
hurt and distant from you when you talk to me that way." Come
from a position of bodily strength with upright posture and both
feet on the ground. Speak in a polite but firm tone of voice,
and avoid accusation or criticism, which your mate may see as
a character assault. In that case, your mate will put up defenses,
likely counterattack, and the conversation will deteriorate. Keep
your statements short and to the point, and resist the temptation
to defend or explain yourself in response to countercharges. End
the dialogue if it doesn't go in a positive direction. Don't fall prey
to yet another hostile exchange that will be blamed on you.

Be forewarned: abusers often derail any attempt at productive
discussion to resolve issues. Many believe they are always right

and disregard other points of view. They stand righteous as they persecute their mates to build their own self-esteem. So let go of expectations that confrontation will bring constructive change in the abuser right away. Until abusers face their demons, own their toxic behavior, and commit to transformation, they will not listen.

You may choose to issue an ultimatum to split up the relationship if your mate's behavior does not improve. When emotional batterers have something important to lose, they are more likely to make an effort to change. On the other hand, he or she may escort you to the front door. If you give an ultimatum, be ready to see it through.

Defying an emotional batterer can be risky and difficult. So prepare for your confrontation by getting informed about what you're up against. Talk to a therapist who specializes in emotional abuse and read recommended books on the subject. Have a safety plan in place and ask close friends, family members, and other people you trust for their support and encouragement. Abusers often respond to resistance with violent retaliation. Take any threats seriously. You may need to exit the house quickly, so prearrange a safe place to stay for yourself and your children.

When you find your voice and draw personal boundaries between you and your mate, get ready for the scorn of others. They either aren't aware of the emotional violence in your relationship, or they have been led to believe that you are the one who causes the strife.

The good news is that refusing to take the abuse interrupts the cycle of intimate partner abuse. Nonengagement in the abuse sets you on a course to develop new and healthier ways to relate to your partner. You can't control the abuse, but you can control how you react to it.

Leaving an Abusive Mate

It takes courage to leave an abusive mate, especially when you're in a weakened emotional state caused by the abuse. The situation can be compared with the plight of the frog that is placed in a pot of lukewarm water on the stove and stays put, unaware that the water is gradually reaching a boiling point and will destroy him.

Some people stay because they believe it's the admirable thing to do, or they don't want to be seen as failures. They may wish to honor their marital vows or prevent a broken home, even if it requires self-sacrifice. They may defer separation until the kids are grown. Others stay because their abusive mates convince them no one will have them, or worse, they will be homeless and financially destitute. Still others stay because they cling to false hope that change will happen in their relationships, but the odds are often stacked heavily against them.

When abused people finally leave their tormentors, they may be motivated by fear of endangering their children if they stay. Parting for the children's sake reduces guilt about breaking up the family. Others split because they anticipate the abuser will commit a criminal act and jeopardize the family's reputation.

Divorce from an abusive partner is a special challenge when navigating through a legal system in which authorities don't readily understand or acknowledge emotional abuse. Abusers use the same tactics on legal experts that they use on their mates. Sometimes legal representatives are emotionally abusive in their own right and take advantage of their clients' hardships.

Whether or not you leave an abusive partner is a personal choice. If you stay in the relationship, you will need to learn healthier ways to cope with the abuse. Make no mistake, however; if your mate's objective is to control you by any means, you are not safe and neither are your children.

When abusers move on to new relationships, it's not likely they will be less abusive, although they will try to convince you otherwise. New partners must fight their own battles against emotional abuse. As you did, they will make the choice whether to challenge the abuse or live with it.

If you decide to exit, take heart. Many women and men have left abusive relationships and are much happier alone or with new partners who treat them well. They build new lives and find healthy relationships. No longer in a noxious environment, they regain freedom to grow and enjoy life, usually more than they had imagined.

SAFETY PLANNING

Anyone who lives with an abusive partner must have a safety plan, whether the abuse is emotional or physical. The plan should include the following:

- a safe place to go any time of the day or night, preferably near by and that can be reached on foot
- a suitcase handy and ready for use
- emergency phone numbers: police, fire department, emergency medical technician (EMT), hospital, family physician, ambulance, shelter, crisis hotline
- phone numbers for supportive family members and friends
- secret money in reserve that is easily accessible
- cell phone that is accessible and in working order at all times
- extra set of house keys
- extra set of car keys
- car in working order at all times or other accessible method of transportation
- community resources

CHAPTER SEVEN

Treatment

PSYCHOTHERAPY FOR THE ABUSED AND THE ABUSER

If this book makes you realize that you are in an abusive relationship, the obvious question is, "What can I do about it?"

The short answer is to get help, whether you decide to leave or stay and work on the relationship. The longer answer involves psychotherapy with a licensed professional therapist who is qualified to treat emotional abuse issues. Either way, find support through your health care, social, or religious and spiritual communities.

Treatment for the abused usually begins when he or she seeks individual therapy for depression, anxiety, disturbing thoughts, or desperate behavior. There may be symptoms of post-traumatic stress syndrome, such as anxiety, headaches, stomach ailments, irritability, outbursts of anger, memory loss, or lack of concentration. Commonly, people in abusive relationships have been to physicians for medical issues and were not screened properly for emotional health.

In therapy, it will take time for abused women and men to realize what has happened to them. Their shame, guilt, self-doubt, and self-deception may have overshadowed the truth about their circumstances. Therapists can help the abused understand the impact of their mates' oppression and how and why the abused may have enabled the mistreatment. The abused will identify and release their deeply painful emotions, make constructive changes in their thoughts and behavior, and work toward recovery. Group psychotherapy can be a powerful adjunct to individual work.

For abusers, the first line of treatment is group psychotherapy led by a therapist who is skilled in treating abusive people. Group therapy with other abusers is one of the most effective ways for abusers to comprehend the magnitude of their harmful behavior. Abusers, however, will typically deny culpability and resist treatment. They may believe their conduct is justifiable. They may fear facing their emotional pain and their partner's empowerment over them. Overcoming such formidable obstacles to change is possible for abusers, but not probable without their participation in a treatment program and their lifelong commitment to change.

Couples counseling can be hazardous when emotional abuse is present. Abusers often fake character qualities they don't have, cover up the abuse, and use information in therapy to exploit their mates. Therapists with insufficient skill in treating emotional abuse issues are reluctant to designate victim and attacker and may unintentionally cause secondary trauma for the abused client.

When couples opt for relationship counseling, it's critical that they work with a therapist highly skilled in treating emotional abuse in couples. Also, it can be problematic for both the abused and the abuser to use the same therapist for their individual counseling.

When the relationships of abusive people end, in many cases they will seek other mates who will accept their behavior, at least temporarily. Abusers often choose to move on to new partners rather than commit to the hard work required to transform their mentality and gain the ability to have healthier intimate relationships.

A very important point to remember: those who abuse don't deserve to be trusted until they've earned it. Abused partners may prematurely gain hope that their relationships will improve when their abusive partners show the slightest indication of remorse and desire to change their ways. Abusive partners, however, must demonstrate repeatedly and over time that they have truly changed and are worthy of trust.

QUESTIONS TO ASK POTENTIAL PSYCHOTHERAPISTS

Finding the right psychotherapist can be a daunting task. Knowing which questions to ask potential therapists will help you find the right fit for yourself and your partner.

You may already have a therapist that you trust. If not, it's important to interview new therapists to make sure they have expertise in treating emotional abuse issues.

First, ask close friends and loved ones to recommend a therapist and search through your resources. Identify a few therapists who appeal to you and make an appointment for a phone interview with each one so that you can ask them the following questions:

1. Do you treat people who have been in emotionally abusive relationships? (With or without physical abuse)
2. What qualifies you to treat people who have been in emotionally abusive relationships?
3. Can you explain some of the deceptive tactics that emotionally abusive people use against their mates?
4. Can you explain some of the ways that emotionally abusive people hide their behavior and present a different image to others?
5. Can you explain some of the reasons why people are abusive to others?
6. Can you explain some of the reasons why people get involved with emotional abusers?

7. Are you qualified to treat emotionally abusive people? (If therapists say yes, ask them about their methods of treatment.)

8. Can you provide referrals for therapists skilled in individual therapy and group therapy for emotionally abusive partners?

9. Do you treat couples when one of the partners is emotionally abusive? What are your qualifications to treat couples when emotional abuse is present in the relationship?

10. Do you have any personal experience with emotional abuse? (Therapists disclose their personal experience only if they believe it is in the best interest of their clients, so they may choose not to answer this question.)

After completing your phone interviews, make an appointment with the therapist whose answers make you feel most comfortable. Take the time to find the right therapist for you. The therapeutic relationship is key to making progress in therapy.

AN INSIDE LOOK AT GROUP THERAPY FOR EMOTIONAL ABUSE SURVIVORS

Group psychotherapy is a powerful method of healing for emotional abuse survivors. If you are a survivor, I encourage you to attend a group led by a qualified counselor who is experienced in group therapy and treating emotional abuse survivors.

Groups bring together people who are up against similar challenges in their intimate relationships. They share feelings and experiences and receive support and encouragement from others in the group, so that they no longer feel alone. Members get relief from their torment and gain hope that they can make a difference in their lives.

The size of the group is usually five to ten members, and the length is typically ninety minutes to two hours. The groups are held weekly or every two weeks for at least six months, but may be ongoing.

The following general questions provide some idea of the types of issues covered in therapy groups. In group, the issues are directed toward each member's personal experience.

1.   Are there specific, individual character traits in people that predispose them to get involved with emotionally abusive partners?

2.   How does family background and sense of self play a role in getting involved with an emotionally abusive partner?

3.   Why do people ignore red flags early in their relationships with abusive partners?

4.   What are some of the main indicators early in a relationship that a person might be abusive?

5.   Why is it sometimes difficult for people to recognize abusive behavior in their partners?

6.   How do people who are abused contribute to an abusive relationship?

7.   Identify and discuss some of the ways people emotionally abuse their partners.

8.   What makes a person take the blame for his or her partner's emotionally abusive behavior?

9.   What happens when the abused attempt to talk about their concerns with abusive partners?

10. How do emotional abusers respond when their abused partners try to express their feelings?

11. How do abused people feel about themselves when they are in an abusive relationship?

12. Do people who are abused by their partners typically have a pattern of abusive relationships?

13. Why do the abused tolerate feeling discounted and disrespected in their relationships?

14. Why do the abused make excuses for their abusive partners when their friends and family members advise them to stand up to the abusers or leave them?

15. What effects do emotionally abusive relationships have on the abused partners?

16. How do abused people contribute to their own abuse?

17. What effects do emotionally abusive relationships have on the *abusers* when their partners accept the abuse?

18. Can the abused stand up to their abusers and stop the abuse? If so, how?

19. How does standing up to emotional abusers and not tolerating abusive behavior affect abusers?

20. What are some safe ways for abused partners to leave their abusers?

21. Can emotionally abusive people change? If so, what do they have to do to stop being abusive?

22. What happens when abusers are allowed to continue their abusive behavior?

23. What effect does an emotionally abusive relationship between parents have on their children?

24. What effect does an emotionally abusive relationship between intimate partners have on their extended family members?

25. What effect does an emotionally abusive relationship have on the abused one's other relationships?

26. Why are people emotionally abusive to others?

27. Can an abused person heal from the trauma of being in an emotionally abusive relationship?

28. What are some of the main ways abused people can heal from abusive relationships?

29. What other types of relationships (other than intimate partners) can be emotionally abusive?

30. How do other types of emotionally abusive relationships affect those on the receiving end of the abuse?
31. What are some ways to prevent being emotionally abused in any type of relationship?
32. What personal changes do emotional abuse survivors need to make to be capable of having a healthy relationship?
33. How do emotional abuse survivors avoid getting involved with another abusive partner?
34. What are the main aspects of a healthy relationship between intimate partners?
35. How will emotional abuse survivors know that they are ready for a healthy relationship?
36. How can emotional abuse survivors help their children heal from having an emotionally abusive parent?
37. How can emotional abuse survivors teach their children to avoid getting involved with emotionally abusive people?

Groups also provide role models for successful coping with difficult relationships and allow members to realize opportunities for change and recovery. The group leader and members observe how other members react in social situations and provide valuable feedback. Members can learn and practice ways to protect themselves within the security of the group.

Women and men in the group acquire deeper self-knowledge, the tools to improve their situation, and the courage to handle tough issues successfully. They learn to take back their power to make healthy choices and get control of their lives.

Epilogue

"The most common way people give up their power is by thinking they don't have any."

- Alice Walker

You may have concluded from the book's acknowledgments that I had more than one encounter with an emotionally abusive person. You might ask: "If her partner was abusive and she left, why did she get involved with *another* abusive partner? Didn't she learn anything?" Well, no, in truth, I didn't. That's because, at the time, I carried the same dysfunctional way of thinking about others and myself into my next relationship. I didn't have the presence of mind to learn more about myself and certainly didn't have a language to help me recognize and describe emotional abuse. Painfully unaware of what was happening, I repeated the experience.

When I set out on a quest to understand my involvement with abusive people, my most startling revelation was that *I* was a significant part of the problem. Even though a little voice inside my head kept saying, "This isn't right," I didn't honor my feelings and intuition. If I had, I would have made better choices.

As I learned more, I realized I had to develop a solid relationship with myself before I could have the relationship I wanted with another. I discovered I had the power all along to take control of the circumstances and protect myself; I just didn't know how to use it. When I understood what had happened to me, emotionally abusive people lost their influence on me, and I found healthy relationships with truly loving and trustworthy people.

During the years I have been with my second husband, I see how vastly different life is when I'm with a partner who nourishes and supports me. I feel fully alive and have made much progress in becoming the person I want to be. Every day holds passion and promise.

In writing this book, it is my fervent wish that I have helped you gain the insight and inspiration you will need to free yourself from the burden of harmful relationships. Step into the light. I'll see you there.

Amy Lewis Bear
February 2014

An Invitation

The author of this book invites you to share your personal stories and your own words, phrases, and examples to describe emotional abuse tactics, effects, and contributors. Please send them to charmtoharm@heartwisecounseling.com. Your submissions may be used, anonymously, in future editions of this book or in other forms of media intended to help others in similar situations. Thank you for sharing your experiences.

Resources

Ablow, Keith. *Living the Truth: Transform Your Life Through the Power of Insight and Honesty.* New York: Little, Brown and Company, 2007.

American Psychiatric Association. *Diagnostic and Statistical Manual of Mental Disorders*, 4th ed. Washington, DC: American Psychiatric Association, 2000.

Bancroft, Lundy. *When Dad Hurts Mom: Helping Your Children Heal the Wounds of Witnessing Abuse.* New York: The Berkley Publishing Group, 2004.

———. *Why Does He Do That? Inside the Minds of Angry and Controlling Men.* New York: The Berkley Publishing Group, 2002.

Braiker, Harriet B. *Who's Pulling Your Strings: How to Break the Cycle of Manipulation and Regain Control of Your Life.* New York: McGraw-Hill, 2004.

Buttafuoco, Mary Jo. *Getting It Through My Thick Skull: Why I Stayed, What I Learned, and What Millions of People Involved with Sociopaths Need to Know.* Deerfield Beach, FL: Health Communications, 2009.

Crompton, Vicki, and Ellen Zelda Kessner. *Saving Beauty From the Beast*. New York: Little Brown and Company, 2003.

Engel, Beverly. *The Emotionally Abusive Relationship: How to Stop Being Abused and How to Stop Abusing*. Hoboken, NJ: John Wiley & Sons, 2002.

Evans, Patricia. *The Verbally Abusive Relationship*. Avon, MA: Adams Media, 2010.

Forward, Susan, and Joan Torres. *Men Who Hate Women and the Women Who Love Them: When Loving Hurts and You Don't Know Why*. New York: Bantam Books, 1986.

Gilbert, Elizabeth. *Committed: A Skeptic Makes Peace with Marriage*. New York: Viking Penguin, 2010.

Hare, Robert D. *Without Conscience: The Disturbing World of The Psychopaths Among Us*. New York: Guilford Press, 1993.

Hay, Louise. *You Can Heal Your Life*. Carlsbad, CA: Hay House, 2004.

Hirigoyen, Marie-France. *Stalking the Soul: Emotional Abuse and the Erosion of Identity*. New York: Helen Marx Books, 2004.

King, Jeanne. www.preventabusiverelationships.com

Loring, Marti Tamm. *Emotional Abuse: The Trauma and Treatment*. San Francisco: Jossey-Bass Publishers, 1994.

Martinez-Lewi, Linda. *Freeing Yourself from the Narcissist in Your Life*. New York: Jeremy P. Tarcher/Penguin Group, 2008.

Miller, Alice. *The Drama of the Gifted Child: The Search for the True Self.* New York: Basic Books, 1997.

Miller, Alice. *The Truth Will Set You Free.* New York: Basic Books, 2001.

Rosenberg, Marshall. *Nonviolent Communication: A Language of Life.* Encinitas, CA: Puddle Dancer Press, 2003.

Stern, Robin. *The Gaslight Effect.* New York: Morgan Road Books, 2007.

Stout, Martha. *The Sociopath Next Door.* New York: Broadway Books, 2005.

Weitzman, Susan. *Not To People Like Us: Hidden Abuse in Upscale Marriages.* New York: Basic Books, 2000.

Index

A

Abusive parents 21
Acceptance 39, 106
Accusations 37, 43, 44, 50, 65, 158, 168, 169
Affairs 44, 120, 122, 125
Ambiguous intent 18, 40, 41
Ambushing 18, 69
Amping up 85
Anger 8, 16, 23, 27, 46, 74, 75, 85, 87, 88, 102, 103, 129, 140, 141, 142, 145, 171, 178, 185, 186, 196
Anxiety 4, 16, 146, 148, 149, 155, 156, 159, 163, 164, 168, 173, 186, 196
Apology 27, 169
Arguments 146, 177, 178

B

Blame xx, 9, 15, 28, 37, 40, 42, 56, 57, 58, 63, 75, 77, 80, 82, 89, 102, 112, 126, 130, 132, 135, 139, 148, 154, 158, 167, 171, 172, 181, 182, 188, 189, 200
Blindsiding 86
Blocking personal growth 114
Blowing bubbles 70
Body aches 161, 173

Body language 27, 80, 98
Boomerang 18, 87
Brooding 88
But, love 18, 61

C

CAD magnet 18, 139
Catching the flu 18, 171
Cause and effect dynamic xx
Change xviii, 12, 15, 16, 20, 22, 24, 25, 45, 56, 61, 66, 71, 75, 95, 108, 112, 114, 117, 125, 142, 146, 166, 167, 175, 176, 185, 190, 193, 194, 197, 198, 201, 202
Chasing your tail 18, 143
Cheating 3, 18, 96, 120, 121, 191
Children xvi, 12, 21, 27, 28, 29, 44, 45, 46, 49, 58, 62, 63, 64, 67, 77, 80, 81, 89, 100, 103, 107, 112, 114, 115, 117, 120, 123, 124, 125, 133, 136, 137, 138, 142, 143, 154, 155, 162, 165, 171, 173, 185, 187, 191, 193, 194, 201, 202, 207
Cloak and daggering 18, 42
Cobwebbing 18, 33
Communication 67, 122, 128, 192, 208, 209

Friends xiii, xv, xvi, xvii, 4, 5, 6, 7,
9, 12, 13, 16, 25, 39, 40, 44,
52, 58, 62, 67, 72, 76, 86, 90,
103, 121, 122, 128, 130, 131,
132, 133, 152, 156, 162, 165,
167, 169, 174, 175, 183, 187,
189, 191, 193, 195, 198, 201

G

Gambling 54, 124, 125, 163, 190
Gaslighting 18, 49
Gastrointestinal distress 173
Gender xi, xvii, 28
Going down with the ship 18, 174
Going underground 63
Golden chains 159
Group psychotherapy xii, 197, 199
Guilt 4, 16, 25, 40, 57, 64, 194, 196
Guilting 64

H

Harnessing 18, 116
Headaches xiii, 16, 159, 173,
178, 196
Healing 196
Honesty 19, 37, 207
Hooked on hope 18, 175
Hostility 28, 50, 56, 77, 85, 89, 91,
94, 98
Hothead 18, 91
House of mirrors 18, 177
Hovering 107
Humiliation 5, 127, 134, 147

I

Ignoring indicators 18, 141
Indicators 3, 18, 36, 141, 200
Individual therapy 196, 199

Insecurity 103, 148, 154
Internalizing criticism 18, 149
In the dark 18, 108
Intimidation xvii, 19, 85, 96, 129
Intuition 4, 7, 11, 16, 23, 25, 42,
139, 171, 203
Invalidation 4
Isolating 18, 133, 169
Isolation 63, 123, 169

J

Jekyll and Hyde 18, 52
Jokes 6, 52, 56, 79, 88, 182, 185
Judging a crook by its cover 18, 142

L

Leaving 26, 66, 127, 155, 194
Limpathy 18, 53
Lost in the woods 125
Lying 22, 36, 54

M

Making a scene 18, 134
Maligning 135
Manipulation 19, 22, 207
Masking 18, 168
Master-at-arms 109
Midnight rider 92
Mimicking 18, 161
Mock-eyed 18, 72
Mocking 18, 110
Mousetrapping 18, 55
Muddled 18, 150, 151
Muzzled 18, 152, 153

N

Nausea xiii

Printed in the United States
by Baker & Taylor Publisher Services